The
Headcount
Solution

The Headcount Solution

HOW TO CUT COMPENSATION COSTS
AND
KEEP YOUR BEST PEOPLE

N. FREDRIC CRANDALL, PH.D.
MARC J. WALLACE, JR., PH.D.

with

BARBARA B. BUCHHOLZ
MARGARET CRANE

McGraw-Hill

New York   Chicago   San Francisco   Lisbon   London
Madrid   Mexico City   Milan   New Delhi   San Juan
Seoul   Singapore   Sydney   Toronto

The McGraw·Hill Companies

Library of Congress Cataloging-in-Publication Data

Crandall, N. Fredric.
  The headcount solution : how to cut compensation costs and keep your
best people / N. Fredric Crandall and Marc J. Wallace, Jr. ; with
Barbara B. Buchholz and Margaret Crane.
    p. cm.
Includes bibliographical references and index.
  ISBN 0-07-140299-3 (hardcover : alk. paper)
  1. Employee retention. 2. Personnel management. 3. Cost control. I.
Wallace, Marc J., 1944- II. Buchholz, Barbara Ballinger. III. Crane,
Margaret. IV. Title.
  HF5549.5.R58 C72 2002
  658.15'53--dc21

                                    2002152685

1 2 3 4 5 6 7 8 9 0 DOC/DOC 0 9 8 7 6 5 4 3 2

ISBN 0-07-140299-3

This publication is designed to provide accurate and authoritative information in regard to the subject matter covered. It is sold with the understanding that neither the author nor the publisher is
engaged in rendering legal, accounting, or other professional service. If legal advice or other expert
assistance is required, the services of a competent professional person should be sought.

> *—From a declaration of principles jointly adopted by a committee*
> *of the American Bar Association and a committee of publishers*

This book is printed on recycled, acid-free paper containing
a minimum of 50% recycled de-inked fiber.

McGraw-Hill books are available at special quantity discounts to use as premiums and sales promo-
tions, or for use in corporate training programs. For more information, please write to the Director of
Special Sales, Professional Publishing, McGraw-Hill, Two Penn Plaza, New York, NY 10121-2298. Or
contact your local bookstore.

Contents

Preface

We talk to our clients frequently. They have repeatedly told us that managing through a business crisis and holding onto the people needed for survival is the single most difficult issue confronting their companies today. It seems to be the topic that keeps many executives up at night, and it has created many challenges for us as consultants. It is a dilemma that "cuts" both ways: how do you cut costs while at the same time keep your best people?

We wrote this book to help companies solve this dilemma. Working with companies in both good times and bad, we have assisted in critical downsizing as well as growth decisions. Some companies have succeeded in maintaining the human capital they need over the long term, while others have failed. Winners have engaged in decisions quite different from losers.

- Winners remain mindful of human capital and keep its value as a high priority when making cost-cutting decisions.

- Winners follow consistent policies during expansion and contraction. They have a game plan ready when the crisis strikes. They are not caught off guard.

The single most important thing to take away from this book is a formula that will allow you to reduce costs when necessary *and* retain the people you will need for the future. We will share with you a seven-step process and practical, adaptable tools to help you quickly decide upon the skills and people you need for long-term success.

We have devoted our careers to a balance of consulting, research, and teaching. Over the years much has remained the same. A constant has been and will always continue to be the need to apply sound judgment to the solution of business problems. We have attempted to provide our readers with such judgments, appropriate for the fast-changing and challenging contemporary environment we face.

Acknowledgments

We dedicate *The Headcount Soultion* to the hundreds of clients and professional colleagues who have supported us and whom we have served over the past 25 years. Our clients have truly been the source of our inspiration and our colleagues have provided us with invaluable guidance. The list is huge, but special thanks go to Nancy Reardon, formerly with Borden, Inc., and now with Comcast; Karen Shuttenberg, of Borden, Inc.; Steve Fazio of Nissan Motor Corporation; Jean Alden of Rich Sea Pak; Dwain Beydler of the Memphis Regional Chamber; John Riordan, formerly of SONY Electronics; Tom Collinger of Northwestern University; John Bremen of Watson Wyatt; Maggie Coil; Rob Wolcott of Northwestern University; Bill Hass of Teamwork Technologies; Howard Risher; and Marc Auster.

Kelly Hyman has worked closely with us in the development of ideas and analyses that led to *The Headcount Solution.* In addition, she has assisted in the research, provided a needed reality test when our ideas got too far out, and provided good counsel all along the way. Paul Schindler, of Schindler Technology, is a partner who has developed the technology allowing us to translate our tools into powerful software. Paul Cherner, with Altheimer & Gray, has been a legal beacon for us to follow in understanding the legal ramifications and implications that one must take into account when making human capital decisions. He has provided advice, counsel, and tools that have been incorporated into the book. We also appreciate the contributions of John DiFrances, John Morrison, Gary Fallert, and Lisa Spathis.

We are grateful to the fine staff of WorldatWork, the professional association dedicated to knowledge leadership in compensation, benefits, and total rewards, for partnering with us in the research that went into this book. Anne Ruddy, Executive Director, has provided strong support and resources all along the way. Lane Michelle Abrahamsen directed the survey discussed in Chapter 2. Additional support was provided by Don Griffith and Ryan Johnson.

Our friends at McGraw-Hill deserve special note. Bill Faris, a longstanding professional associate, introduced us to McGraw-Hill. Richard Narramore, our editior, helped immensely in the original development of themes and chapters, as well as shepherding the manuscript to production.

Finally, we thank Iris Nason and Tracy Scimeca for assisting us in the preparation of the manscript. Their day-to-day support (and a fair amount of criticism) is greatly appreciated.

The Headcount Solution

PART ONE

The Headcount Dilemma

CHAPTER 1

Why the Easy Solution to a Business Crisis— Layoffs—Is Not Necessarily the Best Solution

KEY PRINCIPLES

- Most companies will eventually face a business crisis that requires drastic cost reduction, possibly including layoffs. In this crisis, the main goal is to cut costs without losing your organization's best people.

- The way layoffs are typically carried out ignores the high costs associated with losing human capital. Preserving human capital should remain a high priority for a company, even in a business crisis.

- The solution to a business crisis may involve layoffs, but only after other cost-cutting measures and alternative work arrangements have been implemented.

INTRODUCTION

"We've got to cut $5 million out of the budget, and we don't have time to do any significant analysis. Use intuitive skills, talk to some department heads, decide who the key people are and who is most expendable," said the CEO of a large manufacturing company to his key operations officer.

"But, but . . .," the vice president of operations stuttered.

"There's no debating this. Give them decent severance packages, good recommendations, and some outplacement help to find another job. As head of this company, I know what this business needs to survive. It's fewer people's salaries and benefits. We'll get by; that's all there is to it. I want to see a list by the end of the week."

When businesses are faced with a bad economy, declining sales, or falling profits, the conversations in the presidents' offices often sound like this, though the specific numbers may change. It's the no-guts, no-glory school of cutting heads. Sometimes it's a few hundred, often it's several thousand, and it can reach as many as 5000 or 10,000 for larger corporations. Many company heads believe that having fewer employees is the fastest way to shore up their bottom lines. Corporate loyalty may go by the wayside, but by removing a $30,000 employee here and a $50,000 one there, multiplied by 100, 1000, and 10,000, a business may be clearly on the way to a recovery.

As easy as this "meatball surgery" may seem, it is an oversimplified and potentially disastrous approach to balancing costs and revenues. A company may need to downsize staff because of specific competitive pressures causing a business downturn or it may be caught in a general recessionary environment. These are real problems that sometimes require layoffs. The company needs to cut costs and cut them quickly. But the old approach of simply lopping heads no longer works because so much has changed in the last 10 to 15 years about the workplace and people who are at work today.

Most companies now employ people who have critical business knowledge—human capital—that is not easily replaced. No successful company can survive without a solid base of experts with industry-specific information in many fields, whether it's legal, manufacturing, or marketing expertise.

In a downsizing there is a sizable risk that the wrong people will be let go—the ones who have the most significant proprietary intellectual capital. In the desperate rush to cut costs, leaders may mistakenly dismiss the very people that will help them recover. For instance, a midsized company laid off an accountant on a Friday because it didn't have enough work to justify keeping him. Unbeknownst to the powers that be, he had quietly taken on the tasks of troubleshooting the firm's computer server and internal network. This was not a formal part of his job description. He was a nice guy and loyal employee who never asked for remuneration or recognition that he was helping to keep the system up and running. When there was an e-mail, software, or server problem, he simply dropped what he was doing when needed to correct it.

The Monday after he was dismissed, his presence was sorely missed. Colleagues had problems retrieving their e-mails, customer requests piled up, and some data processes stopped cold. Management was frantic to figure out who would fix the problems. The company ended up with a service contract that cost more than the laid-off employee's salary. Moreover, the response time from the outside firm was far slower and its quality far diminished. Many companies make similar mistakes and lay off the wrong people in their rush to cut costs.

An additional problem with traditional downsizing is that employees may be so upset at their dismissal that they head straight to the nearest competitor or sabotage the firm in some way before they depart. Together, these tough problems constitute the headcount dilemma. This book—*The Headcount Solution*—is about how to resolve these problems.

We wrote this book after years of helping clients grapple with issues such as downsizing and staff reductions. Working with companies in the face of expansion as well as contraction has helped us learn from the difficult and sometimes gut-wrenching situations that leaders of companies face when they must decide whom to keep and whom to terminate. In many cases time has not been on our side. We have had to assist clients in making snap decisions in the face of disaster. In other cases we have had the time and resources to conduct a cool dispassionate analysis of a business crisis. Our goal in both situations has been the same: to preserve the people, their skills, competencies, and leadership capabilities to put the company back on an even footing.

Facing the reality of downsizing and restructuring a business is always a sobering, difficult experience. Every turn seems painful. Moving forward is an uphill battle. However, the seven-step headcount solution is a simple, straightforward way to cut costs and keep the best people.

THE DOWNSIDE OF DOWNSIZING

Traditional downsizing doesn't work anymore because the nature of work has changed. Knowledge work has replaced industrial work, and the two kinds of work are as different from each other as the work in the industrial economy was from work in the agricultural economy it

Table 1-1
Differences between Industrial Work and Knowledge Work

	Industrial Work	Knowledge Work
Management Style	Command and control	Dialogue and empowerment
Skills and Competencies	Physical	Intellectual
Labor Market Conditions	Ample supply of low-wage labor	Scarce supplies of expensive labor
Employee Investment	Low	High

replaced 100 years ago. What's valuable now is the information in people's heads rather than the labor of their hands.

This dramatic change cuts across all levels of an organization and requires a new kind of management thinking, summarized in Table 1-1.

MANAGEMENT STYLE

Management styles have changed over time. The industrial style of management gradually evolved from the turn of the twentieth century up to the 1990s and can be characterized as a hierarchical leadership run by "command and control." Leadership started at the top, and workers were closely supervised. Workers did as they were told and were responsible and accountable for a few closely related tasks.

A breakdown began to occur, however, as work has gradually shifted to an information economy. No longer can a command-and-control mentality supervise sophisticated knowledge, as it once did with physical labor. Employees themselves control much of what is accomplished. And as workers expand the breadth and depth of their skills, today's management style has adapted and become faster-paced in a more intellectually based environment. Command and control have been replaced by dialogue and empowerment. Managers need people who are more autonomous. When a company cuts or lays off an empowered work force today, the ability to get work done is lost.

SKILLS AND COMPETENCIES

Ten or twenty years ago, an assembly-line worker was required to exercise a few physical skills. An automobile assembler might engage repeatedly in five closely related steps to mount an assembly to a chassis. Once mastered, the work became routine and redundant.

Now, intellectual skills supersede the physical component of jobs regardless of the industry, be it financial services, technology, government, health, or legal. Today that same automobile assembler works as part of a team with the intellectual skills to work across an entire process, transforming materials into a finished product. This might include occasionally making managerial decisions and sometimes at breakneck speed. This process has allowed decreased costs while increasing productivity and quality.

LABOR MARKET CONDITIONS

In the industrial economy, employers faced fairly homogeneous labor markets. Labor was cheap and interchangeable. When revenues shrunk, employers quickly adjusted by laying off people until demand returned and then rehired the same people or others.

Again, this is no longer feasible. Labor markets are much more fragmented by specific skills, which are often based on intellectual capital. Finding employees with the right knowledge is much harder and expensive, even in down economies. Ask any manager if labor is hard to find and most still answer "not really," but "smart labor is still really tough to find."

INVESTMENT IN EMPLOYEES

Labor markets with ample inexpensive industrial labor do not require much investment to recruit or select. They demand sheer physical labor, which can usually be learned in a few hours.

In contrast, knowledge work requires high levels of intellectual capital. But this can take years to hone, is expensive, and is hard to find. To cope, management often finds itself caught in an undulating cycle of continually investing time and money to recruit, train, retrain, and retain capable staff, depending on which way the economy is heading. If management lets people go during a downturn, only to discover it needs similar employees later, the cycle begins again. So do the math. In the end the costs are far greater than if the organization had controlled firing and hiring initially. The financial effects are shocking: The one-time cost of replacing a laid-off knowledge worker may equal as much as two to three times the annual salary of the original employee.

In addition to finding knowledge workers, who are in short supply, training new hires also takes money and time, sometimes as long as several months to a year. Productivity is low during such training periods, both for the new employees and those training them.

Finally, losing human capital often means losing "mission-critical" skills that enable a company to implement its strategy and distinguish itself from the competition. For example, Ritz-Carlton delivers superior customer service and accommodations to appeal to travelers, who are then willing to pay premium prices. Federal Express bases its reputation on the capability to complete speedy on-time deliveries to beat other delivery services. Employees must possess a particular set of skills to maintain Ritz-Carlton's and Federal Express's competitive advantage. If they leave the company, voluntarily or involuntarily, the company's ability to execute its strategy is compromised.

So what has really changed? Individual skills and competencies that knowledge workers need in the information economy require far greater intellectual content, more time to develop and maintain, and are more ephemeral than those of workers in the industrial economy. If companies accept these facts and regard employees as human capital, they will view them as less expendable.

Historically, employees were considered short-term variable costs. As revenues and profits dropped, the immediate reaction was to cut employees. Today employees should no longer be considered short-term costs. The human capital they contribute is key to the company's long-term survival. They should now be considered long-term assets rather than expenses, whether the economy heads up or down.

At the same time businesses have to be profitable. So in a business crisis company heads find themselves caught in a headcount dilemma, with the need to cut costs while retaining valuable human capital.

HUMAN CAPITAL AND LAYOFFS: RECENT HISTORY

Between 1996 and 2000 the U.S. economy experienced two important trends, indicating how layoffs have become a natural feature of
the economy. (See Figure1-1.) On one hand employment increased
significantly. More than 2.5 million jobs a year were added between
1996 and 2000. At the same time and over the same period, mass
layoffs became consistent, averaging more than 1 million in over
5000 companies per year. This combination of job growth and layoffs
demonstrates how dependent companies have become on using
layoffs as a management tool. Companies in effect were rebuilding
"on the go," responding to growth needs by bringing aboard new
talent, and at the same time shedding the skills that were no longer
required.

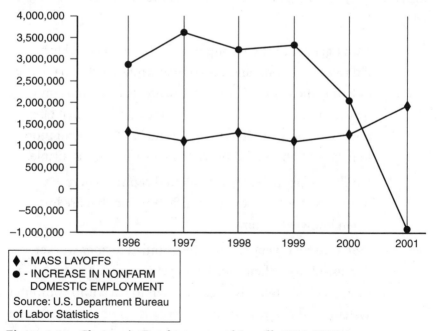

Figure 1-1   Changes in Employment and Layoffs 1996–2001

The recession of 2001 represented a major reversal, or "twist," in the labor market. Mass layoffs surged from 1.2 million a year to 1.7 million in 2001. Coupled with a steep decrease in new hires, organizations were caught in a bind. Those recently hired with the much-needed cutting-edge skills became the first to be cut: last in, first out. As a result companies saved money and propped up the bottom line but paid a significant price. The very knowledge worker skills that were needed most were lost. Proactive companies have learned from this mistake and are beginning to employ a number of cost-cutting methods prior to, instead of, or in conjunction with layoffs to preserve their mission-critical skills.

A SUMMARY OF WHAT NOT TO DO

Before proceeding to the headcount solution, leaders must understand the risks of falling back on the tantalizing allure of old solutions. Here's what not to do:

1. **Don't get rid of the wrong people.** Move too quickly by the old rules for layoffs, and the company might fall into the trap of letting the wrong people go. Corporate heads may only realize this as business returns and the firm lacks that talent pool. The company goes to rehire and has to pay a lot more to find the right staff, if the right people are even available.

2. **Don't lose proprietary intellectual capital.** There are hidden costs of company-specific training that are lost when knowledge staff is cut.

3. **Don't invite revenge.** Some disgruntled former workers dismissed from their jobs try to get revenge and retribution. Laid-off staff have been known to hack into computer systems and destroy customer records. In one case a former employee created a customer relations nightmare by blan-

keting the customer base with embarrassing e-mails. Don't invite revenge by implementing layoffs mechanically and heartlessly. Take the time to communicate to the organization why layoffs are unavoidable and treat laid-off workers with respect.

4. **Don't let fear and isolation take over, which is a sad but common executive response.** Focus your attention on restoring profitability and saving the organization.

ALTERNATIVES TO LAYOFFS

Reducing the number of "heads" in a company is not the best or only way to trim costs. It may meet short-term objectives but could short-change your organization in the long run. Some staff may need to be cut, but only those whose critical competencies are not vital to maintain the organization's mission.

This book discusses many other strategies company heads can deploy to reduce compensation costs without losing the critical human capital needed to sustain competitive advantage both now and in the future.

Two alternatives to layoffs are critical to the headcount solution. The first is to trim overall compensation costs. The second involves alternative work arrangements.

TRIMMING COMPENSATION COSTS

There are many ways to reduce compensation costs before conducting layoffs. The following 10 approaches will be discussed in detail in Chapters 5 and 7:

1. **Offer voluntary severance.** Offer an incentive to employees to voluntarily leave the company.

2. **Offer early retirement.** Allow employees nearing retirement age to take an early out that lets them retain substantial retiree benefits.

3. **Shorten the work week.** Cut out overtime and/or reduce the work week for hourly staff and reduce their total pay proportionately. Be careful that the Fair Labor Standards Act is not violated.

4. **Implement a mandatory pay cut.** Require everyone to take an across-the-board cut in pay, including top management.

5. **Offer stock options in lieu of pay.** Grant employees stock options instead of some part of their current pay or in place of a pay increase. Although not as popular as a few years back, stock options can offer an incentive to remain in a company if a rebound is expected.

6. **Reduce perquisites.** Remove expensive perks such as company cars, expense accounts, subsidized lunches, and golf club memberships.

7. **Reduce or eliminate 401(k) contributions.** Reduce the dollar contribution and/or match to qualified retirement plans.

8. **Reduce or suspend annual pay increases.** Cancel all or part of planned across-the-board pay increases.

9. **Reduce or suspend bonuses and incentives.** Cancel all or part of planned bonuses and incentive payments. Replace them with bonuses contingent on turning around the business.

10. **Implement a hiring freeze.** Suspend hiring new people for the foreseeable future.

These measures alone may not solve the entire cost problem, particularly in labor-intensive firms where employee costs often account for

60 percent or more of total operating expenses. More needs to be done, but these approaches should be taken first.

ALTERNATIVE WORK ARRANGEMENTS

Alternative work arrangements should be considered as well. They accomplish cost reduction yet preserve the skills and competencies needed to compete in the short and long term. These include the following four approaches that will be fleshed out in Chapters 5 and 8:

1. **Job/skill sharing.** Reducing staff to a part-time status and combining jobs into groups for sharing assignments.

2. **Contracting arrangements.** Changing the status of regular employees to a contractual status for part- or full-time work.

3. **Furloughed offsite "Net" workers.** Furloughed employees on limited salary who communicate periodically (e.g., weekly) with their supervisor or team via a telework arrangement.

4. **Temporary assignments.** Special assignments for a specific period (e.g., 3 months) working at a reduced time commitment.

Alternative work arrangements ease the blow. These methods retain vital employees and keep them productive but at a reduced level of involvement and compensation. Some of these approaches are cutting-edge, such as putting employees on furlough and having them stay in touch by laptop computer. Other solutions such as job/skill sharing have been used for decades but often for the benefit of the employee's lifestyle rather than as a way to contain costs. Getting employees to agree requires delicate conversations of why their skills are still sought but to a lesser degree for economic reasons. These issues will be considered in Chapter 8.

IMPLEMENTING THE HEADCOUNT SOLUTION

The headcount solution for cutting compensation costs involves seven steps that are covered in Part Two of this book. These steps can be taken quickly and will leave the organization with a foundation for recovery that will help win competitive battles in the future. The headcount solution allows companies to preserve work, retain human capital and knowledge, and cut costs at the same time. Some people may still lose their jobs and some may have to be relocated, but overall the headcount solution will set a company on a path for an increased return on investment, sustained value of its stock prices, and opportunity for profitable growth.

The headcount solution takes a company from the beginning of a crisis through recovery by cutting compensation costs and retaining the human capital to survive and thrive in the future. Figure 1-2 is an overview of the process.

It begins by preparing employees for what is to come with a comprehensive communications plan. Then it puts the company on a path *to plan* for the three rounds of cost cutting. This includes the basic cost cutting and economic analysis where alternative scenarios are prepared and compared. It results in putting cost cutting budgets into place. Once this is done a consideration of who to cut and who to keep, including a human capital analysis, comes into play.

The company is now prepared *to initiate* the three rounds of cost cutting. The first round involves across-the-board cost cuts that

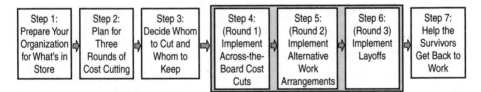

Figure 1-2 The Headcount Solution

concentrate on voluntary separations and reduced compensation costs without involuntary layoffs or forced reductions in the work force. Next comes alternative work arrangements, including a number of ways to cut compensation costs by restructuring work, again avoiding involuntary separations or layoffs.

The last round involves the implementation of layoffs, which will be minimized by the previous two rounds of cost cutting. And the final step involves helping the survivors get back to work.

Following these seven steps will not only reduce layoffs, but it will also ensure that the company has gone through the paces to retain critical human capital. Layoffs alone don't work; they provide a false sense of security. Research over the last 15 years shows that companies that lay off employees to get costs in line with revenues rarely improve on their return on investment or assets.[1] And they never regain the stock price they had before the layoffs.[2] Following the headcount solution will take you on the road to a healthy rebound and recovery.

TEN HARD-WON LESSONS: BEST PRACTICES FOR DOWNSIZING

The 10 lessons learned from the headcount solution that follow will make the journey easier: They represent the best practices of the companies the authors have worked with and researched.

1. See for example, Wayne F. Cascio, "Downsizing: What Do We Know? What Have We Learned?" *Academy of Management Executive*, 1993, Vol. 7, No.1, pp. 95–104; James R. Morris, Wayne F. Cascio, and Clifford E. Young, "Downsizing After All These Years: Questions and Answers about Who Did It, How Many Did It, and Who Benefited from It," *Organizational Dynamics*, Winter, 1999, pp. 78–87.

2. See, for example, Darrell Rigby, "Look Before You Layoff," *Harvard Business Review*, April 2002, pp. 20–21, for a comparison of cost-cutting layoffs to company strategy and stock performance.

1. BEGIN WITH A SIMPLE AND DIRECT PLAN

The plan must clearly state where the company is headed and how it will resolve the crisis. You won't need anything fancy, but you will need a plan that:

- Sets explicit cost reduction goals.
- Outlines specific steps for achieving the goals.
- Assigns clear responsibility for achieving the goals.
- Sets explicit deadlines for each step.

Remember that the plan will not happen by itself. It must be actively managed to completion, like any other important project.

2. MAKE SURE SENIOR LEADERSHIP IS CAPABLE AND COMMITTED

The headcount solution is not something senior managers can order up and expect to happen with no further involvement on their part. Senior management must be prepared to provide the following throughout the effort:

- Visible participation in meetings and announcements at key junctures.
- "Walking around" time with employees to share information and support.
- Monetary and administrative resources necessary to conduct the headcount solution.
- Personal accountability and ownership of the good and the bad effects of the process.

3. CREATE INCENTIVES TO MOTIVATE AND KEEP PEOPLE THROUGH THE CRISIS

Uncertainty and risk must be replaced by an incentive to reach the goals of the plan and place the company on even footing. The incentive should be a cash award if at all possible. The plan should have no more than a 12-month horizon, and it should focus everyone's efforts to reach the goal.

4. MAKE ACROSS-THE-BOARD "COMPENSATION COST" CUTS BEFORE MOVING ON TO ALTERNATIVE WORK ARRANGEMENTS AND INVOLUNTARY SEPARATIONS

The first round of cost cutting should focus on reducing costs without laying off personnel. There are 10 cost-cutting alternatives described in this book that can generate a significant part of the cost reduction goal. In making the cuts be sure to communicate the following to all affected employees:

- Why we are making the cuts.
- How these cuts will save jobs.
- How long we can expect the cuts to stay in place.

5. MAKE SURE YOU FOLLOW ALL LEGAL AND REGULATORY GUIDELINES

When employment laws get violated, the cause is rarely a conscious decision made by someone. The most frequent cause is sloppiness — not following guidelines or inconsistent application of policies. Make sure that all managers involved in the headcount solution:

- Are well versed in their accountabilities under employment laws.
- Act consistently with respect to all policies and procedures.
- Act with sensitivity and compassion.
- Document all their decisions, including the analyses carried out to assess whom to cut and whom to keep.

Most employment law experts suggest that you have a snapshot of employees before and after cuts are made. If the comparison of the two appears to hit a protected group disproportionately, make sure your actions are defensible in terms of the business relatedness of your decisions and assurances of consistency in practice.

6. FIND WAYS TO KEEP GOOD PEOPLE WITH ALTERNATIVE WORK ARRANGEMENTS

Alternative work arrangements are an excellent means of reducing cost while not losing critical people. They require flexibility on the part of management and employees to implement. Take the time to think outside the box. Find creative opportunities for job sharing, for example. Don't be afraid to cross occupational lines when cross-training people to share activities or take on work beyond their traditional job description. When considering cross-training, think of the following:

- Are there any unnecessary, non-value-added activities that I can cut out of a person's work?
- What parts of a person's job could be shared by another or combined into another position?
- Are there any activities that are done daily now that could just as effectively be done once a week or once a month?

Don't fall into the trap of thinking that you don't have the time to entertain these ideas. We're not talking about a massive process reengineering project here. Rather we are urging you to take a few hours to engage in triage and address where you can quickly gain efficiencies that will get the costs out quickly.

7. CONDUCT LAYOFFS AS A LAST RESORT

Some layoffs will be necessary in almost every situation. The headcount solution does not entirely do away with the need to conduct them. Our solution does, however, minimize their short- and long-term negative impacts. They should be minimized and treated as a last effort rather than the first.

We recommend that you follow these guides to getting the most from layoffs while minimizing negative impacts:

- Be truthful about the inevitability of some layoffs from day one. Don't lead employees into a false sense of security that the headcount solution will allow us to avoid layoffs.

- Make sure that employees see and experience the steps preceding layoffs. Assure, for example, that all are aware of the across-the-board compensation costs that have been cut — cost-cutting that has saved jobs. Make sure that everyone knows their role in the alternative work arrangements that are deployed.

8. REMEMBER THAT EMPLOYEES MAY HAVE GOOD IDEAS ON HOW TO CUT COSTS, SO INCLUDE THEM IN THE PROCESS

Employee involvement is a key ingredient. Don't make the error of keeping the bad news from people in an effort to save them discomfort. The worst punishment for employees is to know that something is afoot but not know exactly what.

Employee involvement means three things. First, it means early, open, and continuous communication. Second, it means asking for opinion and feedback. Third, it means meaningful engagement in the process. It doesn't take much time, for example, to brainstorm cost-cutting ideas.

Employee involvement in the headcount solution will yield the following benefits:

- Better decisions because you are using several heads rather than one.
- Commitment to decisions because the choices are the products of joint analysis and decision making.
- Surer and faster implementation because there will be no surprises. People will already know what's going to happen and why. They will already have worked through the "how will this affect me" anxiety and will be committed to the course of action.

9. ACT BOLDLY, QUICKLY, AND DECISIVELY

The headcount solution will test leadership qualities. A leader cannot avoid the issues and still be successful. The headcount solution demands that the company leader:

- Waste no time in putting off painful decisions.
- Personally deliver the bad news to employees, laying out an assessment of the situation in all its details.
- Demand a quick pace by setting aggressive deadlines for specific accountabilities.
- Stay on track with decisions once made.

10. TURN ATTENTION TO MOTIVATING THE SURVIVORS AS SOON AS POSSIBLE

Life will go on. You must show leadership by setting a positive example for those who remain after the layoffs. They are the people who will take the journey with you—the people who will turn your business around.

If you don't take action quickly, a "survivor syndrome" will set in. Sufferers will feel guilty: "Why me?" Many will become cynical: "What's the use? I'll probably be cut in the next round of layoffs!" Imagine trying to unleash creative energies and risk taking when people are suffering such a malaise.

Motivating the survivors will require you to:

- Honor those who have left—acknowledge their contribution.

- Emphasize "that was then and this is now"—focus everyone on the future that lies ahead.

- Reinforce what will happen when the business turns the corner — let people know what that will feel like.

- Attach significant monetary and nonmonetary incentives to specific recovery milestones.

SUMMARY

- In the information economy it's what's in people's heads that counts. If you lose your best people, it will be almost impossible to survive the crisis of a down-turn and the return of profitability.

- Creative reduction of compensation costs and alternative work arrangements should be put in place before layoffs to reduce the number of employees that will have to be terminated.

- The headcount solution is a seven-step process that will cut costs and also retain the best people to help companies successfully recover from a business crisis.

CHAPTER 2

What Companies Are Doing to Cut Costs and Keep Their Best People

---

KEY PRINCIPLES

- Companies are putting many innovative initiatives in place to avoid cutting critical business skills. These include across-the-board cost cutting and alternative work arrangements.

- Across-the-board cost cutting reduces the need for layoffs.

- Alternative work arrangements keep people involved with the company and at the same time reduce costs.

Much of this chapter is based on the results of a research study the authors conducted with WorldatWork, the world's leading not-for-profit professional association dedicated to knowledge leadership in compensation benefits and total rewards, to determine how companies cope with cost-cutting layoffs and at the same time maintain competitiveness. Specifically, the goal was to discover if companies that resort to mass layoffs also try to maintain their human capital by finding alternatives to layoffs. If they do, is the strategy successful? And are companies attempting to keep critical skills and their best people during a layoff? Here are the results.

COMPANIES THAT PARTICIPATED IN THE SURVEY

Almost 6500 companies were contacted for the survey of layoff policies and practices in October 2001. About 19 percent, or 1245, responded. Companies of all sizes were part of those answering, as shown in Table 2-1. The size of companies ranged from fewer than 100 employees to more than 10,000 employees.

The survey included organizations from diverse industries. However, five industries accounted for more than 50 percent of those responding: manufacturing, hi-tech health care, insurance, and wholesale-retail trade. Manufacturing alone accounted for 20 percent, and hi-tech accounted for 14 percent of the survey database.

Table 2-1 Company Size of Survey Respondents

Range	Percentage of Respondents
Fewer than 100 employees	11%
100–999	34%
1000–2499	14%
2500–9999	24%
10,000 or more	17%

The survey responses were almost evenly divided among companies that had conducted layoffs in the last 12 months (49 percent) and those that had not (51 percent).

SUMMARY OF THE SURVEY RESULTS

To avoid cutting into the core of a business' people strengths, numerous initiatives are put into place to retain the best employees. Two approaches are used. The first involves across-the-board cost cutting that ranges from reduction or suspension of pay increases and hiring freezes to actual pay cuts. The more that overall compensation costs can be cut, the fewer number of layoffs will be needed.

The second approach involves identifying people who have important skills and finding alternative ways to keep them involved with the company such as contract workers on temporary assignments or similar approaches. These approaches have worked for hundreds of companies. As the headcount solution unfolds in subsequent chapters, we will relate case studies and experiences of the survey participants as well as simulations drawn from the authors' experience.

HOW MANY EMPLOYEES
ARE AFFECTED BY LAYOFFS?

In most cases a small percentage of the work force was affected by layoffs. About 80 percent of the companies surveyed reported that 15 percent or fewer of the work force were affected by layoffs over the 12 months, as shown in Table 2-2. This may not seem to be a large number, but a layoff of 15 percent may significantly cut right into a company's heart and muscle.

Table 2-2   Workforce Laid Off by Companies

Percentage Laid Off	Percentage of Companies	Cumulative Percent of Companies
1–5 %	44%	44%
6–10 %	23%	67%
11–15%	13%	80%
16–20%	7%	87%
21–30%	6%	93%
31–39%	3%	96%
More than 40%	4%	100%

ALTERNATIVES TO LAYOFFS

The research study split the companies surveyed into those that had and those that had not conducted layoffs over the last 12 months. It tabulated the number of companies that either considered or implemented the 10 types of cost-cutting measures a company can take to reduce compensation costs. As Table 2-3 shows, in every case a greater percentage of those companies that conducted layoffs also implemented or considered initiating cost-cutting measures.

The most popular cost-cutting methods for companies laying off employees were hiring freezes (63 percent), reduction/suspension of annual pay increases (57 percent), and reduction/suspension of bonuses and incentive pay (55 percent). The relatively high consideration of these cost-cutting measures means that companies involved in layoffs looked carefully at all options before moving forward. They considered and weighed a wide range of combinations rather than pursuing only one option.

Alternative work arrangements are a means to offer partial employment opportunities to employees for partial compensation. These include job sharing, temporary assignments, or restructuring work arrangements from regular employment to contract arrangements.

Table 2-3 Cost-Cutting Measures in Conjunction with Layoffs

Cost-Cutting Measures Considered or Implemented	Layoffs Experienced in the Past 12 Months	
	Yes	No
Voluntary severance package offered to Employees	34%	11%
Early retirement package offered to employees	20%	15%
Shorter workweek for all employees	25%	12%
Mandatory across-the-board pay cut	20%	4%
Offer of stock options in lieu of pay	13%	4%
Perquisites reduction (e.g., expense accounts, clubs, etc.)	37%	18%
Elimination/reduction company contribution to 401(k) plan	12%	4%
Reduction/suspension of annual pay increases	57%	30%
Reduction/suspension of bonuses and incentive pay	55%	29%
Hiring freeze	63%	43%

Alternative work arrangements are a way to cut costs and at the same time keep mission-critical skills that the newest hires, the first to be laid off, often possess. The reshuffling of work assignments inherent in such arrangements is a departure from the past and demonstrates the desire of organizations to find ways to retain the best people.

Companies that experienced layoffs within the last 12 months are more likely to have offered alternative work arrangements (Table 2-4). The experience of respondents in the survey differs with each alternative. Offsite Net workers—a new approach to work—are considered or used by fewer than 10 percent of companies in contrast to temporary assignments, which are used and considered by more than 33 percent of companies that have conducted layoffs in the last 12 months.

Table 2-4   Alternative Work Arrangements in Conjunction with Layoffs

Cost-Cutting Measures Considered or Implemented	Layoffs Experienced in the Past 12 Months	
	Yes	No
Job/skill sharing	24%	19%
Contracting	24%	18%
Offsite Net workers	8%	6%
Temporary assignments	34%	22%

THE IMPORTANCE OF HUMAN CAPITAL

A key question asked of survey participants was: "How important do you believe your upper management team feels it is to preserve human capital during times of organizational layoffs?" Answers are summarized in Figure 2-1. The overwhelming response was very important (43 percent). This helps bring into focus the way that companies cope with mass layoffs and the value they place on the preservation of human capital.

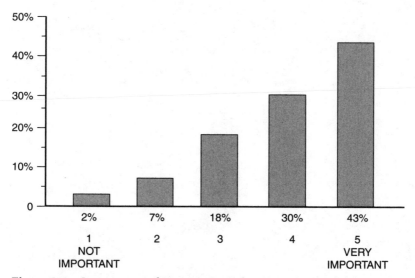

Figure 2-1   Importance of Human Capital to Top Management

SUMMARY

- Creative compensation cost cutting and alternative work arrangements are novel ways companies hold on to critical skills in a crisis.
- The more a company can utilize alternatives to layoffs, the fewer layoffs it will find necessary.

CHAPTER 3

Leadership During a Crisis: How to Maintain Morale and Keep Your Best People

KEY PRINCIPLES

- Senior leadership must have credibility in the eyes of employees to lead through a crisis and beyond.

- Senior leadership should understand the motivation and concerns of employees to motivate them effectively.

- Employees need to understand the future direction of the company and how the crisis will be resolved in order to be positively motivated.

- Senior leadership should lead employees on a direct and simple path to gain their confidence.

- Incentives are required to support the objectives and intentions of senior leadership and reinforce commitment to stay with the company.

HOW TO MOTIVATE PEOPLE TO STAY DURING A CRISIS: THE SIMPLE ANSWER

During a crisis people turn inward. They revert to their strengths—what they know best. They try to protect and preserve what surrounds them. Sometimes this even includes building psychological barricades around the problem to avoid dealing with it. But often in a business crisis, there is a need to reach beyond the old ways of doing things to create a new plan. This is not easy.

Taking costs out of a company to restore profitability may mean resorting to extreme measures, sometimes over a protracted and painful period of weeks and months. Some employees may be asked to leave. Others will be assigned to new jobs or told to assume new tasks. The simple solution to maintaining morale and motivating key people in a crisis is to align everyone's current and future interests. Alignment is the necessary first step. It can best be defined as the mutual understanding among managers and employees of their shared benefits and incentives to work together in the face of crisis and adversity. Additionally, all this must be achieved in an environment where layoffs, separations, and many other milestones and changes will occur.

There are four steps to motivating employees in a business crisis:

1. *Assemble a capable and credible leadership team.* Senior leadership must be capable of leading the company through the crisis. In certain cases work will need to be done to remove individuals who will be roadblocks to a turnaround.

2. *Lead people on a direct and simple path forward.* Work with senior leadership to develop the broad outlines of a recovery plan.

3. *Align everyone's interests.* Consider the broad array of senior leadership and employee motivations. Then zero in on factors critical for survival.

4. *Introduce positive incentives for employees to stay.* Monetary and nonmonetary motivators will have to be offered to keep employees involved.

A CHANGE OF LEADERSHIP IS OFTEN REQUIRED[1]

Many companies that find themselves in a crisis have had some kind of a problem with leadership. To get through the crisis, attention must be paid to two aspects of senior leadership. The first is its capability to lead the company out of the crisis, and the second is its credibility. If the leadership is not capable or not credible, the company will not be able to motivate employees and keep its best people.

A new leadership team is often necessary because a leadership group that has failed in the past may not generate the confidence necessary to motivate and keep critical human capital during the crisis. Moreover, the senior leadership must be in a position to challenge the way things have been done in the past. Senior leadership must not be perceived to have biases toward systems, procedures, and people that are part of the problem. The leadership team must be capable of developing a simple plan that motivates everyone's buy-in and hard work.

A DIRECT SIMPLE PATH FORWARD

If employees are to be motivated to stay for positive reasons (as opposed to fear and insecurity), they must have a clear understanding of the actions management is taking to solve the organization's problems. The message management sends must be concise and clear so that people can direct their activities and adjust them accordingly. They need to

1. Material in this section was contributed by William J. Hass of Teamwork Technologies.

have a sense that everyone has a purpose and a cause. If there is no clear direction, stability will be hard to achieve.

Here's an example of what a company should not do. In response to a falloff in sales, one company's senior leadership conducted an analysis of the marketplace and arrived at the conclusion that 15 separate initiatives were required to capture lost sales and initiate new growth. When the 15 plans were presented, managers and employees became confused. Without a clear, concise message, the employees didn't understand the real priorities. They did not know how to direct their activities. In a short time, when business did not improve, people began to lose faith in management. At that point some of the best employees started to leave the company.

Borden Foods provides an example of how to communicate a turnaround message clearly in a crisis. Borden manufactured pasta under a number of brand names and operated a manufacturing and distribution business throughout North America. Its presence in the market was threatened by diminished operating margins that endangered the viability of the business. Senior leadership knew it had to take drastic steps to save the business. After conducting a substantial analysis, Borden's leadership focused on streamlining operating costs. The plan that senior leadership created was simple and straightforward: All associates in the company would devote their energies and activities toward reducing the cost to manufacture and deliver pasta to customers for one calendar year. Everything else would be secondary. The message was clear. Everyone knew where they stood, what they were supposed to do, and what results they were expected to produce during the year. Interestingly, everyone also knew that cutting operating costs would ultimately mean that cuts in staff were to come. But the reductions were aimed at a specific purpose with the ultimate benefit to all, whether or not the employees remained with the company. This became much more palatable for the work force.

AVOID THE TEMPTATION TO ACT TOO QUICKLY

There is a temptation to make cuts in payroll before a recovery plan is put in place. This is often done because it demonstrates direct and proactive action on the part of senior leadership. The headcount solution calls for laying off staff as a third and final round of cost cutting. The reason for waiting is that laying off staff before developing a plan may result in cutting the wrong people, demoralizing survivors, and providing for a slow ramp-up time to get back into the market.

ALIGN EVERYONE'S INTERESTS DURING A CRISIS

Aligning interests is a three-step process. The first step is understanding employee motivations to stay and leave during a crisis. The second step is understanding the reasons for senior leadership to retain or let go employees. The third step is aligning employee and senior leadership interests to create a plan for the future.

UNDERSTAND WHY EMPLOYEES STAY DURING A CRISIS

There are three reasons an employee would want to stay during a crisis:

1. *"I need a job."* This reflects fear about the future, uncertainty about obtaining employment elsewhere, and the need to pay the mortgage, leading people to hunker down and not want to move.

2. *"I am truly loyal and committed."* This attitude reflects faith that is unshaken. No matter what happens or what has happened in the past, some employees remain faithful. This

is the group of employees who would need to be physically removed from their desks.

3. *"I see a future with the company."* Employees are convinced that staying with the company will be beneficial because of the direction it is headed and because the end of the crisis appears to be in sight. This type of motivation is essential for success in the future. It embodies a willingness to meet challenges with a desire to succeed. In this case, the fear of losing a job is overshadowed by a positive commitment to the future.

UNDERSTAND WHY EMPLOYEES LEAVE DURING A CRISIS

There are typically three reasons someone would not want to remain at a company during a crisis:

1. *"I have lost faith in the company."* This is the inability to see a path forward that makes sense to the employee or the inability to see where he or she fits into future plans. Losing faith can result from an employee losing confidence in leadership or simply, as an insider, not believing the company has a chance to succeed. In either case there is a failure by senior leadership to reach the employee. Senior leadership can have a major impact on employees either losing or gaining their faith.

2. *"I have good options for my career and I should take advantage of them now."* It is critical for senior leaders to carefully establish incentives to keep employees, sending a clear message about their value to the enterprise. Those employees who perceive their options as "better" in the marketplace will go elsewhere.

3. *"This is a good time to leave."* There is a window of opportunity to take advantage of a severance or a reduction in

work force package. Taking advantage of early retirement (or another benefit) is similar to the second reason for leaving. However, in this case the company is in effect offering competing incentives to stay and to leave. Senior leadership should consider very carefully the incentives it creates for employees to leave or stay.

SENIOR LEADERSHIP'S CRITERIA FOR RETAINING AN EMPLOYEE

Just as employees consider the notion of staying or leaving, senior leadership also weighs options to retain or let go employees. During a crisis, senior leadership is motivated by three reasons to retain employees:

1. *"This job is necessary."* The immediacy of the situation usually results in quick judgments regarding which employees can perform needed tasks. However, senior leadership also needs to ensure that it has the critical human capital—the skills and competencies required for the company to recover and grow. Balancing these two needs requires a human capital review and analysis. (See Chapter 6.)

2. *"We are loyal to our employees."* This attitude can have long-term positive results for an organization. Sometimes, however, there is a down side. Many leaders are not realistic about the true capabilities of employees for the future because they are blinded by loyalty. The service and loyalty of employees should be a high priority during difficult times. However, it should not be at the expense of sound judgment regarding the human capital that will be required for the company's future. Preserving jobs should be a high priority, but maintaining the right combination of skills and competencies should also be given top priority.

3. *"We retain good performers."* It makes sense to try to retain high-performing employees. This is perceived by most employees as a fair way to make layoff decisions. Of course, it does not make sense to maintain employment of poor performers in any case. While senior leadership may be motivated to keep good performers, it begs the question, "Who are the good performers?" Without an effective performance management program or other means of assessing skills, there may be disagreement over past performance or prospects for the future. Senior leadership and management should not jump the gun when deciding which employees best fit the company's future needs.

SENIOR LEADERSHIP'S CRITERIA FOR LAYING OFF AN EMPLOYEE

Senior leadership typically has two motivations to terminate an employee's services:

1. *"This job is no longer needed."* This is the most frequent reason cited when employees are dismissed. However, the motivation of the employer and the message given to the employee are often unclear. Is it the job that is not required or the skills the employee possesses that are no longer needed? If a company does not have a clear path about how to proceed, then senior leadership may retain and terminate the wrong employees for the wrong reasons.

2. *"We terminate poor performers."* Poor performance should be considered at the get-go for termination. But the same issues should be used to identify the good and the poor performers. Senior leadership should not base layoff decisions on past performance without a consistent, fair

method of evaluating individual employees. Otherwise, lawsuits are invited.

OBTAINING ALIGNMENT BETWEEN EMPLOYEES AND SENIOR MANAGEMENT

Attaining alignment is not easy. The combination of all of the motivations of employees and senior leadership during a crisis appear in Table 3-1. There are potentially conflicting motivations.

Employees and senior leadership may be conflicted among themselves and with each other. An employee may not know the company's intent. Or the company may be unsure about whom to keep and what employees will be required to do in the future. The key is to sort through all the potentially conflicting motivations and perceptions. Then leadership should align positive company interests with positive employee motivations by doing the following:

1. *Minimize employee motivation to leave and enhance the motivation to stay with the company.* Develop and communicate a simple straightforward business turnaround plan. This will reduce fear and increase faith in the company's future. It will also provide employees with a frame of

Table 3-1 Motivation to Stay and Leave in a Crisis

	Employees	Senior Leadership
Motivation to stay	"I need a job." "I am truly loyal and committed." "I see a future with the company."	"This job is necessary." "We are loyal to our employees." "We retain good performers."
Motivation to leave (voluntarily or involuntarily)	"I have lost faith in the company." "I have good options for my career and I should take advantage of them now." "This is a good time to leave."	"This job is no longer needed." "We terminate poor performers."

reference to compare against outside opportunities, hopefully placing the company in a positive light.

2. *Focus on the skills and competencies the company needs for future success.* When it comes time to determine whom to keep and lay off, place decisions in a framework of skills and competencies necessary for the company's future. In other words, review the company's future plans and ask the tough questions that define the requirements needed to ensure the plan's success.

At the end of the day, companies want the right people to stay for the right reasons. Unfortunately, at this point in a crisis, many leaders do not know who those people will be. Chapter 5 is a guide through the process.

FINANCIAL INCENTIVES FOR RETAINING TALENT DURING A CRISIS

The most straightforward way to create incentives for people to stay during a crisis is to make their tenure with the company "profitable." There are financial and nonfinancial elements to these incentives. In this section we describe financial incentives, and in Chapter 10 we will go into detail concerning the nonfinancial incentives that are relevant in a crisis.

Financial incentives generally translate into a cash incentive plan. For a short-term situation, cash is a critical vehicle to motivate people to stay. The incentive should also directly tie to important results for the company and align everyone's interests in working toward results. This fourth step in motivating people to stay during a crisis is a capstone on executing the first three steps: A capable and credible leadership team must be assembled and everyone's motivations must be understood and then aligned with a simple, straightforward plan. An incentive will reinforce and support the plan. Putting together an incentive plan involves the following:

1. Start with three or four simple goals for everyone to work on to get the company on a path to recovery.

2. Make the time period short enough to capture everyone's attention, which might be anywhere from 6 to 12 months.

3. Focus on operations or activities that people can actually do that will result directly in the expected changes.

4. Have a set of goals that "roll up" from the lowest level of daily operations to the top level of management. This will get everyone working toward the same ultimate goal. This means that employees working in a plant or production facility will be working on the same plan as senior executives.

5. Provide meaningful financial results for reaching the goal, such as a cash award starting at 5 to 10 percent of each employee's salary for reaching goals and going upward for exceptional results.

Borden Foods followed these five steps in developing its incentive plan during the crisis described earlier. The first step Borden took was to identify a specific set of "challenge" goals that the entire company could embrace. The most important goal for the organization was to raise the level of profit or earnings before interest expenses and taxes (EBIT) were paid. Earnings were computed as sales minus costs of operating the business. This was senior leadership's key responsibility. While everyone in the company in some way contributed to profit, the concept of EBIT was really too abstract for a direct and immediate impact on all employees. Recognizing this, senior leadership determined that the greatest number of employees had an impact on the conversion and distribution costs of the company, whether they worked in a plant, a warehouse, or in the customer service department. Conversion costs included the costs of converting raw ingredients and packaging materials into finished products, not including the actual purchase price of raw materials. Distribution costs included the costs incurred to deliver products to customers and storage. Therefore, specific targets for conversion and distribution costs were set as challenge goals. In addition, the goals for conversion and distribution costs were to be met without a sacrifice in customer service levels.

Looking over the employee population, three groups were established to receive incentives. The first group was the senior leadership of the company. The second group was the professional and technical staff that included marketing and sales, customer service, research and development, human resources, administration, and other support staff. The third and last group included the majority of the employees, those involved in production and distribution facilities throughout North America.

The challenge goals for the plan were allocated differently for each group of employees as outlined in Table 3-2. All of the incentive for senior leadership was based on reaching the EBIT goal. Similarly, 100 percent of the operating employee incentive was based on operations and distribution cost goals. These goals were expressed as the cost per pound of converting raw material into product and the cost of shipping the product to customers. Operations employees had a clear and

Table 3-2 Incentive Plan Design

	Operations:	Support Staff:		Senior Leadership:
Employee Group	Production facilities Distribution facilities	Plant management Sales Support areas		Executives Company management
Incentive Allocation	100%	50%	50%	100%
Performance Measure	Conversion and distribution costs	Conversion and distribution costs	EBIT	EBIT

straightforward input on reaching this goal. Support employees' goals were split evenly between conversion and distribution costs and EBIT. The support staff had an indirect impact on operations and also had an indirect impact on EBIT through their activities. Thus, their goals were split 50/50.

The time period for this incentive plan was one calendar year. To have impact it would take a number of months to establish initiatives to reduce costs and increase profits. At the same time senior leadership recognized that operations and distribution employees needed to receive feedback on reaching cost reduction goals in a more timely fashion. So the decision was made to have monthly measurements and payments on actually achieving the conversion and distribution costs goals. (See Figure 3-1). Interim payments were set for reaching interim objectives on the way to the year-end goal.

The payout for incentives was a meaningful part of total compensation for participating employees. The payout targets ranged from a minimum of 5 percent of base pay for entry-level employees to 40 percent of base pay for senior leadership.

The plan was very successful in capturing the attention of all employees and was a prominent part of the work life of the company. The company was quite successful in dropping operating costs and

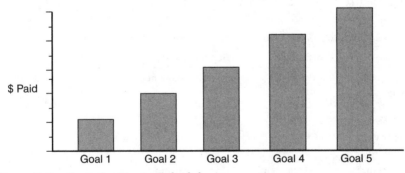

Figure 3-1   Incentive Payout Schedule

increasing profitability over the 12-month period and accomplished most of the goals.

LESSONS LEARNED

The lessons learned from Borden Foods are applicable to other companies involved in a business crisis and attempting to rally the troops at the same time. To revisit them:

1. Put together a simple plan that everyone can understand and work on.

2. Align the goals and objectives of everyone to be successful with the interlocking or cascading goals that "roll up" to ultimate profitability of the business.

3. Ensure that everyone has a financial interest in the outcome.

4. Monitor the goals to ensure they are achieved.

5. Communicate progress along the way.

THE SEVEN-STEP PROCESS

It is critical to motivate people to stay during a business crisis. Once that is done, the hard work to cut costs and keep the best people really begins. Part Two of this book presents the headcount solution. In it the reader is taken through the seven steps necessary to survive the crisis and thrive in the future:

Step 1:   Prepare Your Organization for What's in Store

Step 2:   Plan for Three Rounds of Cost Cutting

Step 3:   Decide Whom to Cut and Whom to Keep

Step 4:   Implement Across-the-Board Cost Cutting (Round 1)

Step 5:   Implement Alternative Work Arrangements (Round 2)

Step 6:   Implement Layoffs (Round 3)

Step 7:   Help Survivors Get Back to Business

SUMMARY

- Surviving the crisis begins with a concentrated effort to motivate employees to accept the challenges that will come.

- Senior leadership should concentrate on keeping the right people for the right reasons.

- The essentials for motivating people to stay are a simple plan, an alignment of interests, and incentives to make it worthwhile to remain with the company.

PART TWO

The Headcount Solution

CHAPTER 4

Step 1: Prepare Your Organization for What's in Store

KEY PRINCIPLES

- Senior leadership must be honest and forthright about the difficulties the organization faces and the cost-cutting steps it may have to take.

- Employees want news delivered promptly and clearly with no important data or facts hidden.

- Employees want to know what will happen to their company in the short and long term as well as what will happen to them and their colleagues.

WHAT'S IN STORE

Once the senior leadership of a business realizes that it faces a business crisis and that painful cost-cutting measures will have to be taken, the first step is to communicate the seriousness of the situation to the organization. Preparing an organization for major cost cutting, whether it will involve layoffs, requires thorough planning, execution, follow-up, and some old-fashioned handholding and compassion.

As managers start to heed the advice about the advantages of the headcount solution and how to implement it, one point becomes very clear. It takes time and effort. Furthermore, there is a great deal of uncertainty in making such drastic changes, and uncertainty fuels rumors and distrust.

There are savvy and considerate methods to communicate to employees what's in store. These include the need for honesty and clarity to get messages across so that everyone hears and understands the same information clearly. Most of these approaches are based on real company situations and experience. Tables are included in this chapter that show what to communicate, which communication channels are best, and any communication programs that should be used. In addition there are suggestions about obtaining input from employees. All these approaches to open and clear communication will help prepare managers and staff for what lies ahead.

THE IMPORTANCE OF HONESTY
AND CLARITY

Organizations have learned that employees want honesty; they don't want to be patronized. If a pay cut, hiring freeze, or layoff is in order, they don't want to be told "I know how you feel." In most cases their bosses do not know how they feel, especially if they were never laid off. However, the manager of compensation at a firm in Maryland was able to be more compassionate with employees when his company conducted the first two rounds of layoffs. He had been through layoffs before at another company, and he found that it was easier to tolerate them a second time. As a compensation manager, he said that the hardest thing to deal with after a first round of layoffs was whether the cuts were deep enough so the company didn't have to go through the trauma of another round.

Employees want to know the facts: why something is happening and the circumstances surrounding the actions taken (e.g., how many people will be let go, when is their last day of work, what is included in the severance packages, whether the company can help get them a job, and if they might be rehired later). Those remaining—the survivors— also want to know whether more cuts are imminent and when. It's important for everyone to be brutally honest.

Honesty is the only way to break bad news. A loan company located in Kansas City, Missouri, doesn't gloss over any news it must deliver but says it straight out. The reason? The goal is the same for each employee: Everyone wants to be able to get moving on their resume, networking, and hitting the pavement running.

People crave strong leadership. Former New York Mayor Rudy Guiliani became a shining example of a good manager who imparted bad news with sensitivity and candor. He didn't pull punches and provided the wisdom of being forthright yet compassionate when he delivered daily reports after the September 11, 2001, terrorist tragedies. He updated the number of deaths, injuries, financial losses, and he shared his thoughts on how to cope. He told what he knew and admitted what he didn't know. As a result he earned the kudos and admiration of a global audience.

David L. Brown, manager of compensation at CNF Transportation in Palo Alto, California, said his company has taken a similar approach. It tries to be open, communicate bad news honestly, summarize the external environment, tell the status of the company, and offer alternatives when it can.

FIVE GUIDELINES FOR DELIVERING THE NEWS

Sharing bad news is never easy, but the following five guidelines can make it less stressful and difficult, both for the messengers—the managers—and those on the receiving end—the employees.

GUIDELINE 1: COMMUNICATE FREQUENTLY TO GET EMPLOYEES IN THE HABIT OF HEARING ABOUT CHANGES IN THE ORGANIZATION

Cost cutting is easiest if employees understand why the changes are necessary in terms of the company's current economic status and the overall economy. Specifically, they want to know how many workers will be affected, in which areas and departments of the company, and at what levels. In a sluggish economy, unfortunately, it is easier to get everyone on board about accepting changes because fewer outside job options exist.

The Employers Association Inc. in Minneapolis, Minnesota, a membership organization of 1700 employers, described its current business issues in the context of the economy and then explained exactly what it was going to do. Susan Eskedahl, CCP, senior manager, said that if the firm had to reduce benefits, it would explain why via one-on-one and departmental meetings.

Another approach to keeping the channels of communication open as the best way to get staff to accept change, in good and bad times, is discussed by Terri Anne Lacobucci, human resources director at International Knife & Saw Inc. in Cincinnati, Ohio. Her company leaders talk with people, with staff face to face, if a crisis arises. For everyday updates, employees are kept abreast of company news through e-mails and postings for those who don't use e-mail. Some may not like so much communication, she said, but at least it's available if they want it. Similarly, at World Now in New York City, the CEO delivers news through a state-of-the-world e-mail message. Some companies use several media channels. One health-care system in Houston deploys an internal newsletter, leadership meetings for management, and updates for all employees.

GUIDELINE 2: DEVISE A CLEAR, CONSISTENT COMMUNICATIONS PLAN TO DISSEMINATE NEWS TO THE ENTIRE ORGANIZATION, SO THERE'S LESS CHANCE FOR RUMORS TO SPREAD

The company has to decide what the news is and who is going to sign off on the information (it can be a group of upper management, the head of the company, a department manager, the public relations department, or the human resources director). The company also has to decide how the news will be imparted based on the type of news—whether it's typical corporate business or an emergency. The firm might call an all-company meeting or choose to disseminate news through a town-hall-style gathering, individual department meetings, company e-mails or memos, or letters sent home (if matters are more sensitive or private).

The specific approach depends on a number of factors, such as the size of the organization, whether employees work at one central location or many, or how employees are use to receiving information. Gathering everyone together when there are thousands of employees or even hundreds at multiple sites may prove too difficult. The Employers Association in Minneapolis, which employs fewer than 100, has the luxury, however, to make decisions at the senior management level and then gather employees into smaller groups for quick dissemination.

Besides size and location, the decision may hinge on the culture of the company. Some corporate heads like to share the news. The director of a security services company notes that his company's strategy is for the head to present a concept in a face-to-face meeting of top management, which is about 15 people, and then to provide the news at that point from the top down to everyone in e-mails. The human resources staff fills in the specifics.

There are four critical protocols that should be part of the communications plan, especially if the announcement relates to a crisis.

Official News Source. During a crisis people don't know who or what to believe. Rumors are rampant. To make sure the company gets its message out to employees, official "news" sources of information should be designated. This is more important today than ever because there are so many ways that news can be disseminated, whether through traditional sources or the Internet. In a one-location company, everything is under one roof. It is relatively easy to manage the communications process. However, with multiple locations potential problems abound. The company must designate how official information will be communicated. The official news source in most companies is either a special designated spokesperson or a communications/public relations department devoted to information dissemination.

The Rumor Hotline. A novel approach that numerous companies use is a rumor hotline, which is a means for employees to verify information heard unofficially. It works through phone and/or e-mail by providing a means for staff to report information or ask questions 24 hours a day. For example, if somebody hears that a plant in Iowa is going to be closed, the person can call the hotline and ask for verification. Usually, answers are promised within 24 hours either by return voice mail or e-mail.

Timing. The most important part of timing is consistency. The company should set expectations regarding how often information will be disseminated. This will focus employees on expected announcements at regular intervals. Once a schedule has been set, it is important to meet deadlines. If not, employees may read unintended meaning into the lack of communication. Even if there is nothing new to report, a deadline should not be missed. An update saying nothing has changed should be reported to allay fears or rumors. This disciplined approach pays off to keep people focused, informed, and ready to build confidence in management and the company. It makes employees feel the company is reliable during a crisis and is taking care of their interests.

Official Channels. Once the company has established official sources and timing, official channels should be designated. This will facilitate clarity on where information will come from and what to watch. Channels include written letters, e-mails, and in-person meetings. Each channel is suitable for a different type of communication. Table 4-1 outlines the spectrum of communications available and employee audiences that are appropriate for each. (Chapter 9 on implementing layoffs provides more detail on how to communicate layoffs effectively.) The media can range from personal one-on-one interactive discussions to broad-based, companywide, one-way communications. The trick is to match the type of message to the appropriate medium. The hardest part is in the middle of the spectrum where group meetings are advised. In this case, managers may need to set up an interactive format but control disruptions from disgruntled individuals who want to take out their frustrations in a public forum.

Communication channels are important because they carry the message managers want to make. Not all channels are equally appropriate for all messages. As the company undergoes up to three rounds of cost cutting, care must be taken to put the right message on the right channel. Table 4-2 summarizes the appropriate messages for each channel.

For changes in personal status such as job assignments or termination, personal meetings and letters are appropriate. If the issues are more applicable to a work group, group meetings will suffice. Finally, mass meetings and other mass media make sense for companywide communications. It also makes sense to combine these channels sometimes. More intimate discussions and meetings will often follow mass communication.

Table 4-1 Channels for Communications in a Business Crisis

Communication Medium	One-on-one meeting	Personal letter or e-mail	Small group meeting	Large group meeting	Mass meeting	Video conference	Newsletter or mass e-mail
Audience	Personal	Personal	Team	Department	Division	Company	Company

Table 4-2 How to Use Communication Channels

Channel	Personal Information on Change of Status	Team or Departmentwide Changes	Companywide Changes
One-on-one meeting	X		
Personal letter or e-mail	X		
Small group meeting		X	
Large group meeting		X	
Mass meeting			X
Video conference			X
Newsletter			X
Mass e-mail			X

Companies use communication channels in a variety of ways. Many emphasize the importance of in-person meetings so questions can be asked and rumors forestalled. Ron Van Iderstine, Dallas' Parkland Hospital's director of employment, said his company opts for face-to face contact rather than to send e-mails. One Ohio company, which tends to direct its news to specific divisions rather than companywide, says that an appropriate manager might travel to each of its six facilities to conduct small meetings.

E-mails or letters are acceptable as generalized information because they apply to a large number of people. Parkland did so when it announced a differential in holiday pay. It sent e-mails and letters, the latter for those without access to the Internet. It has found that multiple channels ensure the word gets out to everyone, whether technologically savvy or not.

Life Cell in Branchburg, New Jersey, a biotech firm with 150 employees, disseminates bad news departmentally whenever possible if several people are affected. If only one person in the department is let go, the boss tells that employee in a one-on-one session. If a large layoff occurs, an all-employee meeting is called, and employees are walked through the decision-making process.

Judy Colyn, human resources manager, cites company policy. Once decisions were made they were discussed at the quarterly Town Hall meetings. Employee questions were answered and morale was minimally affected. In fact, one employee commented she had considered leaving, but after hearing management's thought process and concern for employees, she knew "this is the kind of company I want."

The Communications Action Plan. A communications action plan is the result of choosing protocols and establishing communications channels. Table 4-3 shows what a communications action plan looks like.

The complete communications action plan should be developed before the communications process begins. The action plan puts together official communications, channels, and timing into a coherent framework. For some events specific timing is not known, so managers need to specify expected dates that will be subject to change.

The president of Parkland Health & Hospital System in Dallas, Texas, likes to send letters, as he did when announcing the option of early retirement. The letters were sent to eligible employees' homes.

Table 4-3   A Communications Action Plan

Subject	Communicator	Channel	Timing
We have a company crisis	President	Mass meeting	January 5
Progress on company turnaround	President	Video conference	Monthly
We must reduce the merit pay budget	Vice president of human resources	Mass e-mail	March 10
We will begin a job share program	Vice president of operations	Department meeting	March 10
Job share opportunity	Department manager	One-on-one meeting	March 11–20
We will have to lay off 5 percent	President	Mass meeting	June 1
Layoff discussions	Department manager	Department and one-on-one meetings	June 2–6

They also explained that the organization was not sure whether it might have to conduct layoffs if an insufficient number of people did not come forward and volunteer. The letters were followed up with seminars and counseling to educate workers how the early retirement would work, and a time frame of several months was offered for decisions to be made. Compensation manager Jane Mason said that the tone was positive, and no layoffs were necessary because 200 employees elected to leave.

Finally, it's important that any messages from different departments or levels be consistent. This can be done by gathering managers together and giving them a script that they don't digress from. Managers should practice if they need to once given the information.

GUIDELINE 3: DECIDE WHETHER A MEMBER OF THE HUMAN RESOURCES DEPARTMENT OR A COMPANY ATTORNEY SHOULD BE PRESENT IN THE CASE OF JOB CUTS

Many companies believe that a third party, either an HR member or the firm's lawyer, should be excluded from the discussion unless trouble is expected. It can set the wrong tone and make the meeting more intimidating for everyone.

Other companies disagree. Some think having such a person present will make the news easier to present from the get-go, make it easier to respond to specific questions, and make it easier to disseminate information about timetables.

A third option is to have such a third person available once the initial news is provided so that questions can be directed to the right parties within the organization quickly.

To avoid any legal entanglements, some companies have a termination scripted so the manager conducting the layoff is not derailed in any way. The statement, usually drafted by a corporate attorney, is short and to the point.

GUIDELINE 4: PROVIDE THE FACTS NEEDED AND NEVER MAKE A PROMISE THAT CANNOT BE KEPT 100 PERCENT

Employees want to know specifics no matter what the subject. If there is a pay freeze, they want to know how long it will last. If there is a change in overtime policy, they will want to know the specifics. If there is one round of layoffs, there might be more, and employees should not be promised that terminations will stop. Most important, managers delivering news should be prepared with backup facts and should have rehearsed giving answers to questions typically asked. In advance they can write a script, practice answers, and anticipate questions.

Telling the truth to employees always works best whether the news to be shared is good or bad. If bad news isn't communicated to employees, it can turn into rumor and innuendo. Moreover, employees may lose trust in leadership. They may feel disengaged in the company. As a result morale may sink and productivity may drop. But when company leaders are honest, treat people with respect, are open about corporate problems, and share facts as fully as possible, employees typically want to help in whatever way they can. This is especially crucial for employees who remain after the layoffs have taken place.

GUIDELINE 5: FOLLOW UP BY PERIODICALLY CHECKING THE PULSE OF EMPLOYEES AND SEEING WHETHER SURVIVORS CONTINUE TO REMAIN WITH THE COMPANY

A sense of relief may develop once the messages have been shared among those who haven't been cut, but that euphoria or optimism may quickly wane if the business doesn't turn around and more employees must be cut. Good supervisors manage by walking around, talking to staff, finding out how they feel not just on the days when messages are delivered but afterward and on a continuing basis.

Additional steps are to meet informally in small groups, meet in one-on-one sessions, have coffee or lunch with those in a department, and keep lines of communication open.

HOW TO OBTAIN INPUT FROM EMPLOYEES

Input from employees is critical. It will help quell rumors, provide high-quality ideas, and improve morale. Employees want their input to be heard and considered, not discounted. But input must be handled carefully. It can raise false expectations of changes that will not occur, and it can create cynicism. How many times have you heard, "They ask for our opinion but never take it"? Managers must set expectations around involvement that are realistic. For example, if employees are in a group meeting to brainstorm cost-saving meas-ures, the manager might say, "We are soliciting your input today. We will consider every idea that is raised. However, management alone will make decisions. It will take us about 3 weeks to arrive at a deci-sion. Once we have done so, we will let everyone know."

Input can be derived from a number of in-person sources, including one-on-one meetings, focus group sessions that concentrate on one or two topics, and departmental staff meetings. There are other more formal ways of soliciting input like ongoing suggestion programs. Whatever way is developed, it will help keep communications flowing and focus everyone's attention on resolving a business crisis.

Companies should have ways to gather input easily and sometimes anonymously. Suggestion boxes in a hallway or by a water cooler or coffee station make giving feedback easy. Have slips of paper and pens. Or have employees e-mail their suggestions and reward ideas with the equivalent of "frequent-suggestion" points that they can cash in.

By making such events and needs easy, employees and managers are more likely to participate and keep talking to one another more often. Good communication has a domino effect: It adds to more frequent communication.

SOLIDIFY SUPPORT

If a company takes the foregoing advice, it will gradually solidify support from employees. Respect for managers will increase; managers too will respect the owners or heads of the company, and that will trickle down through the ranks.

How do leaders know if this support has been achieved? It is obvious, almost palpable, in the way employees come more enthusiastically to the office, work hard during the day, casually get together and talk about positives rather than negatives, try to take on whatever assignments they can for the good of the company, pull together, not blame anyone, and know that all is being done to improve the bottom line.

Casual conversations, formal conversations, questionnaires, focus groups, and surveys can be taken periodically to ask employees what they think about what's going on, what more they want done, and what they want to see less of. Have a point-person at the company who handles these data and walks the hallways too so that people know who to go to if questions or problems arise.

WHAT NOT TO DO

All of the work to develop an effective communications plan can be undone by just a few misstatements that fuel the rumor mill or contribute to lack of confidence. Here's what managers should avoid doing at all costs:

1. Managers should not respond to any questions from employees unless they are absolutely sure of the answer. They should say, "I don't know, but I'll get back to you as quickly as possible with an answer." There should be ample ways to verify information quickly.

2. Managers should avoid giving any employee advance or "inside" information. This is not the time to play favorites with anyone, and it's also unprofessional.

3. Managers should stay away from situations where they are involved in informal discussions that include speculation about future prospects for the company. Even the presence of a manager in such situations could make a faulty impression and fuel rumors.

Employees will scrutinize every statement, nuance, and even the body language of every manager. The sensitivity of the situation calls for clarity, honesty, and maturity from every manager.

SUMMARY

- Managers need to be honest and clear about what is happening to the company and the employees. If they don't know, they need to explain that; if they do, they need to share that.

- No matter how often news is available, managers need to develop systems to provide it regularly to employees and in the best ways possible, such as through e-mails, letters, and one-on-one or group meetings. Otherwise, rumors tend to develop and spread.

- Decide who the point-people are to be on hand to help deliver the news, such as a member of the HR department or a company attorney.

- Have ways for employees to provide their input and get regular feedback so they feel a part of the changes occurring.

Step 2: Plan for Three Rounds of Compensation Cost Cutting

KEY PRINCIPLES

- The headcount solution involves planning for three rounds of action:

  (1) across-the-board cost cutting;

  (2) implementing alternative work arrangements; and

  (3) laying off employees.

- The goal of this planning is to cut the maximum cost while retaining the maximum human capital.

THREE ROUNDS TO CUT COSTS: BASIC ECONOMICS

Whether caused by a downturn in the economy or the need to turn around a troubled company, the single most pressing demand on managers is to get costs out quickly. Consider the division manager of an information systems unit of a troubled company. A new CEO has the mandate from the board of directors to cut costs quickly and turn losses into profits. The division manager receives an e-mail that directs him to cut 20 percent of his annual employment costs of $79.75 million—a total of $15.95 million.

The division manager ponders, "How am I going to cut these costs? Where do I start? What will do the least damage?" His first thought is to initiate layoffs. "Some people (maybe 200 of our division of 1000, or 20 percent) will have to go," he thinks. "Maybe it doesn't have to be 20 percent of the people. Maybe there are some costs I can cut without having to lay off people. How much money are we spending on perquisites, I wonder? Those could be easily cut and they won't cost me talent. But I'm still going to have to cut people. Maybe I can find the highest paid people to let go. That way I can get 20 percent of the cost out with fewer layoffs. But they probably are the ones I can least afford to let go."

The manager's thoughts speak volumes about the economic considerations confronting any leader who has to reduce operating costs. But they are knee-jerk reactions. They don't follow an organized game plan. To act intelligently and in the best interests of the company, leaders in a crisis need to consider the costs that must be reduced and the strategies to accomplish the cuts. The headcount solution calls for a cost-cutting strategy that consists of three rounds:

Round 1: Across-the-board cost cuts. Cutting costs without laying off people.

Round 2: Alternative work arrangements. Finding alternatives to traditional employment that will allow the company to cut compensation costs yet hold onto the mission-critical talent the company needs.

Round 3: Layoffs. If costs remain to be cut after Rounds 1 and 2, laying off those employees necessary to achieve the cost-cutting requirement. Layoffs at this stage are typically smaller than would have been necessary if the company had done across-the-board layoffs as the first strategy.

The manager in this scenario must reconsider what to do after each round of cost cutting.

ROUND 1: ACROSS-THE-BOARD COST CUTS

The information systems division manager estimates costs that can come out in Round 1. First the manager lists current compensation costs:

1. Headcount: 1000 full-time employees
2. Annual salary cost: $55 million
3. Annual Employment (Salary + Benefits) Cost: $77 million
4. Annual overtime: $2.75 million
5. Annual employment cost with overtime (salaries, benefits, overtime): $79.75 million
6. Average annual salary per employee: $55,000
7. Average annual benefits per employee: $22,000
8. Average annual compensation cost (salary + benefit) per employee: $77,000
9. Average tenure: 4 years

Next the manager considers cost-cutting steps that will avoid laying off people. The human resources division (after consulting with several professional HR associations on best practices) advises the division manager to weigh 10 actions commonly taken to lower costs short of a layoff. (These are described in detail in Chapter 7.)

Cost cutting requires planning. It can't be implemented overnight. In certain cases some investigation and analysis are necessary to see if an option is feasible (e.g., early retirements and severance offers). Other steps involve policy at the corporate level and cannot be implemented unilaterally by a division (e.g., stock option grants in lieu of pay increases). In addition the steps require a certain amount of resources to be executed. The manager may contemplate the use of a high-level task force to deal with the issues and make final recommendations. The task force must be organized and chartered. It might take more time for such a process to work, but the decision will have more buy-in for the tough measures the manager is about to take. Finally, a large organization may demand consistency of action across major divisions and units to ensure internal equity. The efforts of multiple division heads may be coordinated and assisted by a corporate HR function.

The manager builds a spreadsheet (see Table 5-1) to estimate the costs he can cut in Round 1:

The manager concludes that he can remove $5.77 million in costs in Round 1. He also notes that implementing these steps will be critical in terms of getting that cost out at this point. Other essentials include:

1. He must be explicit about when the costs will come out. The spreedsheet covers the costs that will come out this year.

2. He must make sure not to violate any employment laws, regulations, or contracts in taking the costs out.

3. He must communicate well, explaining why the costs have to come out and the benefit in terms of saved jobs.

Table 5-1   Round One Cost Savings

Action	First Year Savings (Benefit)	Comment
1. Five employees take voluntary severance	$332,100	Five employees @ $77,000 annual total compensation cost-severance cost*
2. Five employees take early retirement option	$332,100	Five employees @ $77,000 annual total compensation cost-severance cost*
3. Cut out overtime	$2,750,000	Overtime is $2,750.000
4. Mandatory pay cut	$0	No pay cut at this time
5. Perquisite reduction (k)	$550,000	1% of a $55,000,000 total annual salary cost
6. Reduced 401k contribution	$550,000	1% of a $55,000,000 total annual salary cost
7. Reduced annual salary increases	$550,000	1% of a $55,000,000 total annual salary cost
8. Reduced annual bonuses	$550,000	1% of a $55,000,000 total annual salary cost
9. Hiring freeze	$154,000	Two positions @ $77,000 annual total employment cost per employee per year
	Grand total first year savings	$5,768,200

*The savings fot the first year will be impacted by severance cost. Each employee is offered a severance package equal to two weeks pay for each year with the company and accrued vacation. Average tenure is 4 years and average vacation time is 2 weeks. Average weekly salary is $1058. Thus, the package is $10,580 for each employee.

4. He must identify those costs that not only should come out now, but also would always stay out. Future year cost savings will be higher due to the one-time costs for voluntary severence.

5. He must establish the conditions under which the costs removed can be reinstated.

ROUND 2: ALTERNATIVE WORK ARRANGEMENTS

"Well, I've pared $5.77 million off a $15.95 million problem," the manager concludes. "I still have a little more than $10 million to go!" he agonizes. The second round requires that the manager look for alternatives to traditional employment that will allow him to get compensation costs out while retaining the mission-critical talent he will require to meet his division's business objectives. He lists some possible alternatives (described in detail in Chapter 8):

1. **Job/skill sharing.** "Surely there is some staff who would be willing to share a full-time employment (FTE) slot. Think of two software engineers, as an example," he ponders. "Each has a salary of $55,000. If both were willing to share one-half of a job, I could shave $55,000 off $110,000 in salary cost and still retain the benefit of both for their expertise."
    There are several practical considerations to make such a work arrangement, however. First, how many people would want to share a job? It isn't something a company can force on people. It takes people willing to cooperate with others and share joint accountability for results. In addition the manager will have to prepare department heads and supervisors for managing the arrangement so it does not interfere with the division's work.

2. **Contracting arrangements.** The manager has another thought. "We have any number of technicians and engineers who are great troubleshooters, real aces. But we can't justify full employment. We really don't have that many problems all the time. But when we do have a problem, we need help—and fast. There are probably people who would be willing to work on their own as independent contractors. A number of managers have already told me of many engineers who are thinking about going out on their own. They could contract back to us. We'd be their first major client, and they would be free to add other clients as they see fit as long as there are no conflicts of interest."

He adds, "It won't be a free lunch. We'll have to pay a higher hourly rate in consulting fees than we're paying in salary right now. Also, there may be some minor severance costs such as payment for accrued vacation. But we won't have the benefits cost, and we will be free to use as little or as much of their time as we need."

There's another consideration here, he knows, remembering an earlier conversation with the corporate human resource officer. He notes, "The IRS has already cracked down on us for abusing contracting. Just calling someone a contractor does not remove that person from employee status, absolve us of our duty to pay social security taxes, and withhold income tax. We'll have to be careful to make sure that people who go on contract will truly be contractors in the eyes of the law. The contractors have to be independent of us. That means they supply their own tools. They work independently of the company. They are not under the direct supervision of our managers. Finally, they are free to take on other clients."

3. **Offsite Net workers.** This is something I could combine with job and skill sharing, he surmises. "We already have a virtual private network (VPN) in place." He decides that he should try to find 30 people who would be willing to reduce their time on the job by one-quarter and work from home.

In addition he knows that if he equips those going part time with telecommuting equipment (laptops, distributed network software, high-speed cable access), he can free office space. "If I could get rid of half my space, I would save a great deal in lease costs. Unfortunately, leases are extremely complex to change."

Reducing leased space takes a great deal of lead time and depends on the timing of the lease itself. Doing something may take the discretion of corporate staff and is beyond the manager's immediate control. Although it's a good idea, the manager doesn't have the time to deal with this solution now.

4. **Temporary assignments.** Finally, a fourth possibility is considered. "We must have some people who are working on critical projects. For example, managers have told me that they are upgrading systems software. Even if we can't justify full-time employment for them, perhaps they would be amenable to working on the projects to completion with no guarantee of continued employment after their conclusion. We could adopt a wait-and-see posture, hoping to find something for them at that time. All of these are great ideas," he notes, "but I wonder how much they cost to implement?" He makes a list of each alternative work arrangement and considers the benefits in terms of costs saved and the cost of implementing the alternative. (Table 5-2).

The manager produces a spreadsheet to capture the overall cost reduction potential of the four alternative work arrangements. The spreadsheet appears in Table 5-3.

He believes that if he can find 50 people, at an average salary of $55,000, who would be willing to share work for the year, he can reduce salary costs by $1.375 million this year. In addition he hopes to find 20

Table 5-2   Cost/Benefit Considerations of Alternative Work Arrangements

Alternative Work Arrangement	Cost Savings (Benefit)	Cost
1. Job/skill sharing	Proportion of FTE salary	Negligible
2. Contracting	Proportion of FTE salary and benefit obligations	Additional cost of salary rate (and minor severance costs such as accrued vacation time)
3. Offsite Net workers	Real estate savings and proportion of FTE salary (if working part time)	Cost of telecommuting equipment and start-up
4. Temporary assignments	Proportion of FTE salary	Negligible

Table 5-3   Cost/Benefit Analysis of Alternative Work Arrangements

Alternative	Comment	No. FTEs	Total Salaries	Impact	Cost to Implement	Net Cost Reduction
1. Job/skill sharing	Save 50% FTE salary	50	$2,750,000	$1,375,000	$0	$1,375,000
2. Contracting	Save 100% of annual total compensation (salary plus benefit) of $77,000. Pay a contracting fee.	20	$1,540,000	$1,540,000	$1,000,000	$540,000
3. Offsite Net workers	Reduce 30 people to 3/4 FTEs. Introduce telecommuting.	30	$1,650,000	$412,5000	$30,000	$382,500
4. Special projects	Place 10 employees on half time and assign to specific projects.	10	$550,000	$275,000	$0	$275,000
	Overall net cost reduction					$2,572,500

staffers who could work on contract to accomplish specific mission-critical services. The net benefit in cost savings for shifting to contractor status would be $540,000 (the $1.54 million in total employment costs—salary plus benefits saved—less the estimated $1 million the manager will pay in consulting fees when the former employees contract back to the company).

He further calculates that putting 30 employees on 75 percent of an FTE and having them work from home will save an additional $382,500 in net compensation costs savings. This is $412,500 in salary costs, less $30,000 to implement, for a net savings of $382,500.

Finally, he expects that the company can place 10 people on special projects at half time—a move that would save an additional $275,000.

"Here's how I can pare an additional $2.57 million," notes the manager, "and still get to hold on to people. Granted, I'll have to put some people on part-time work. But I'm getting to my cost goal," he reflects. "If I can get $5.77 million in Round 1 and another $2.57 million, that's $8.34 million of a $15.95 million problem. Now I've got $7.6 million to go!"

ROUND 3: LAYOFFS

The last resort to reducing operating costs is a layoff. The manager thinks about what can be accomplished. "Clearly, if I lay an employee off, we get the benefit of the reduction in cost of employment (compensation, benefits). But what if I lay the wrong person off? What if we lose talent we need and suffer loss of business as a result?"

These considerations force the manager to look at the consequences of layoffs in terms of four basic areas. As Table 5-4 shows, the term *costs* can refer to short-, and long-term savings, a benefit to the company, and to the short- and long-term costs that need to be incurred to achieve the savings. The latter reflect what the company will have to spend to achieve cost savings.

Most companies usually concentrate on only one of the four elements in Table 5-4: cost savings in the short term. However, such a narrow focus is fraught with peril.

SHORT-TERM COST SAVINGS

The first cost category consists of the costs saved when an employee is laid off. Such cost reduction provides an immediate benefit to the firm and is the category most managers focus on when making layoff decisions. The category consists of the following elements:

- Salary
- Benefits (e.g., health insurance, life insurance, pension contributions, etc.) that can amount to an additional 40 percent above the employee's salary
- Incentives and bonuses

The division manager identifies an employee whose cost of employment is $77,000 per year (including a base salary of $55,000 and other costs, including benefits that amount to $22,000). If he finds 100 of these people, the company can get immediate relief in the form of a $7.70 million reduction in annual payroll costs.

Table 5-4 Benefit and Cost Consequences of Layoffs

	Short Term	Long Term
Cost Savings	Immediate salary and benefits reduction	Salary and benefits if replacements not rehired
Costs Incurred	Severance costs, which may account for 20% or more of short-term cost savings	Staffing, recruiting, and lower productivity associated with rehires

SHORT-TERM COSTS INCURRED

Unfortunately, it's not that easy. Companies conducting a layoff find that there is a price to pay in the short run for getting costs out by actions such as layoffs. These costs are listed in Table 5-5. They find that there are still a number of obligations due the employee being severed:

- Accrued vacation. A majority of employers offer paid vacation each year, and in most cases the vacation benefit accrues throughout the year. An employee who is terminated during a year may have several days of paid vacation coming, and this obligation must be met even if the company separates the employee.

- Cost of outplacement services. Many companies have adopted a policy of providing a terminated employee with the services of specialists who can assist in finding new employment. Such services include counseling, coaching, resume preparation, the use of office facilities, and other support. These costs can range from several hundred to several thousand dollars per employee.

- Severance salary and benefit continuation. Most employers have policies of continuing salary and benefits (e.g., health insurance coverage) for a period of time, often several weeks or more, at the company's expense. The number of weeks offered is based on the employee's length of service with the

Table 5-5   The Real Cost of a Layoff (Short-Term Costs Incurred)

Cost Item
1. Accrued paid vacation
2. Outplacement services
3. Severance salary
4. Total cost per employee separated (total of 1, 2, and 3)

organization. This represents a benefit beyond the requirements of the COBRA law of 1985 that requires employers to
offer group health plans to terminated employees for 18
months (at the employee's expense).

The division manager builds a quick spreadsheet to assess the real
cost of a layoff. He enters the number of employees to be laid off and
their average salary employment cost. He also makes estimates of short-
term costs per employee based on company history and experience. The
output looks like the analysis in Table 5-6.

"So, I'm going to have to spend $1.99 million or so to save about
$9.63 million. The net cost savings will be $7.64 million for the first
year," he concludes. "Okay. Let's see where we are," he examines further.
"I've taken out $5.77 million in Round 1, another $2.57 million in
Round 2, and this round will add another $7.64 million in costs for a
total of $15.98 million. I've just beaten the goal of $15.95 million."

The manager's thinking has not yet reached the long-term cost
consequences of cost cutting and layoffs. The company fully intends to

Table 5-6   Net Short-Term Cost Savings (Benefit) of a Layoff

Annualized Short-Term Cost Saving		
1. Annual total compensation cost/employee	$77,000	
2. Total employees to be laid off	125	
Total annualized savings		$9,625,000
Short-Term Cost to Implement*		
1. Outplacement services/employee	$ 1700	
2. Severance package/employee	$12,000	
3. Accumulated paid vacation/employee	$2200	
Total cost/employee	$15,900	
Total cost to implement layoff		$1,987,500
Net Short-Term Cost Savings (Benefit)		$7,637,500

*Actual numbers are rounded for this example.

be around 5 years from now and longer. All too often in the heat of the crisis, leaders focus on the obvious benefit (reducing short-run costs.) However, they lose sight of less obvious longer term costs that may come back to haunt them in the future. What are some of these longer term economic consequences?

LONG-TERM COST SAVINGS

A layoff results in reduced employment costs in the long term. The benefit will last as long as the company doesn't need to rehire the employees. But what has actual experience been? The majority of companies that lay off employees find themselves back to prelayoff employment levels within 18 months.

What happens? When the cost crisis is over, excessive employment cost has been diminished as a prime issue. Management's attention now focuses on growing revenues, and it is very willing to spend on employment costs to achieve that objective. The reality is that most companies that lay off employees do not experience a long-term benefit from employment cost reduction.

LONG-TERM COSTS INCURRED

The information systems division manager in this narrative is concerned with losing skills and competencies the company will need now and in the future if he lets his best people or the wrong people go. His fears are real. They speak to the equally real but less tangible costs a company incurs when it loses valuable human capital. "If I let Sam go," the manager ponders, "he probably won't be available a year or two from now to rehire. That means I lose all of Sam's know-how." He's right; the company has lost the investment (selection, orientation, formal training, and informal job experience) it made in Sam. These are skills and competencies that must be built all over again when Sam's replacement is hired. The manager lists the hidden costs the company will face when it rehires:

- **Market premium for attracting the separated employee's eventual replacement.** This means the company may find that it has to pay a market premium to attract a replacement, a figure higher than the salary of the severed employee.

- **The cost of recruiting and screening candidates for the job to be refilled.** Most companies that lay off people find themselves recruiting to refill the position within 18 months after the termination. Ads need to be placed, recruiters hired, and even search firms engaged to develop a set of applicants from whom to screen. The selection process also costs money, for example, to conduct interviews, administer tests, follow up with references, conduct physical examinations, and perform other screenings. Such costs would not have been incurred if the company had not laid off staff in the first place. These costs can easily amount to 5 percent of the first year's salary for each candidate screened. A company might spend $12,500 ($2500 each) to screen five candidates to fill a position that pays $50,000 per year.

- **The cost of orienting the replacement.** The new hire can't just pick up where the laid-off employee left off. The new person will need to be oriented to the job and the organization. He or she will have to learn all that is unique about the company, its culture, and its industry. Many organizations provide formal orientation, which adds to costs.

- **The cost of the additional guidance and supervision required during the replacement's initial period of employment.** The new employee costs the company in nonproductive hours while climbing the learning curve on a new job. He or she also requires more guidance, mentoring, and attention than a seasoned veteran. Somebody has to provide the supervision, and that takes time away from other tasks.

- **The lost productivity while the replacement learns the ropes.** Finally, there is an economic opportunity cost incurred. This is the difference between the productivity the company would have enjoyed had it retained the laid-off employee and the productivity of the replacement while he or she is learning the job. How many times have customers patiently waited to be served while a new salesperson was learning the software system? How many times have customers wished they had drawn the seasoned employee?

- **Costs can run up to an amount equal to two or three times the annual compensation of the person laid off** and is a cost above and beyond the annual salary of the replacement.

The division manager builds a second spreadsheet to estimate the long-term costs the company will incur to achieve whatever long-term cost reduction is realized. The output looks like that presented in Table 5-7. All of the elements in Table 5-7 will be incurred as soon as the company replaces the employees it laid off.

Time becomes a critical factor when considering long-term costs savings and long-term costs expended. Most companies laying off staff are back to prelayoff employment levels within 18 months. The longer the time of reduced employment, the better the economics because of the recurring long-term costs savings. But let's say that this company experiences rehires within a year of the layoffs. Now the company has spent $20.6 million in long-term cost incurred to save $7.52 million for a year (see Table 5-6). And that calculation does not take into account less tangible costs that exist, and are just as real:

- Low morale and survivors' syndrome
- Lost innovation

Table 5-7   The Real Cost of Layoff (Long-Term Costs Incurred)

Cost Item	Amount per Employee
1. Recruitment, selection, and orientation expended on the employee who was laid off ($12,500 to screen applicants, $7500 to orient)	$20,000
2. Training investment (based on 5 years' service @ $3000 for training each year)	$15,000
3. Recruitment, selection, and orientation of the new hire as a replacement ($12,500 to screen applicants, $7500 to orient)	$20,000
4. Market premium paid to attract the replacement (assuming the company will bid $60,000 to replace the $55,000 person laid off)	$5000
5. Estimate of the cost of additional supervision during replacement's first year	$5000
6. Economic opportunity cost of lower productivity during the first year (based on the replacement working at 75% of the veteran employee)	$100,000
7. Total long-term cost per replacement (total of 1–6)	$165,000
8. Total long-term cost for replacing 125 layoffs	$20,625,000

- Fear

- Angry customers

- Lost market share

Smart decision making demands the manager to consider all four benefit/cost categories just described. Focusing only on the short-term cost reductions can lead to bad decisions such as laying off the wrong people and spending even more to replace them a short time later. The discipline of considering the plusses and minuses represented by all four categories will lead to the right decisions about whom and how many to lay off and whom to retain.

Managers should take the following steps:

1. Consider how all four cost categories apply to the organization and the particular situation.

2. Recognize that even in the short run, there's no free lunch. It will cost to lay off staff.

3. Don't discount or underestimate the long-term costs associated with layoff actions.

4. Be careful about timing; consider how long the period will be before rehiring. The shorter this period of time, the more you should avoid taking layoff actions.

If these steps are taken:

- Fewer people probably will be laid off.

- Mission-critical people who need to be retained will be identified.

- The negative impact will be minimized, including costs in the short and long run, which provides the opportunity to recover quickly and inexpensively.

RAISING YOUR SIGHTS

This case analysis shows the benefit of the headcount solution. Planning ahead for three rounds of cost cutting, rather than just instituting a massive layoff, allowed the manager to layoff only 125 employees. If he had gone directly to layoffs, he would have had to involuntarily terminate over 250 people to cut $15.95 million in costs.

There will always be situations where labor is relatively inexpensive and easily replaceable and where it makes sense to treat labor simply as a short-term cost. In these circumstances, the headcount solution might not be feasible when a business is in trouble or faces a downturn in a business cycle. Increasingly, however, the economics in settings such as technology, professional services, pharmaceuticals, and lean manufacturing is characterized by investment in human capital. Again, this is where skills remain scarce and in demand, and the company must make a substantial investment in skills and competencies. In these situations, basic economics will force leaders to raise their sights and consider labor not as a cost, but rather as an investment.

SUMMARY

- Managers should always see the amount of costs that can be trimmed in Rounds 1 and 2 of cost cutting before they resort to layoffs.

- For a short recovery cycle, it is easy to see the drawbacks of layoffs as an effective cost-cutting tool because people must be rehired before the long-term benefits are accrued.

- The real cost of a layoff includes selection, recruitment, and training costs for new hires in the future, all of which significantly eclipse short-term savings.

- Layoffs are most effective if employed with other cost-cutting measures and alternative work arrangements that preserve critical human capital.

WORKSHEETS FOR THREE ROUNDS OF COST CUTS

This section contains skeleton worksheets for you to use in making cost/benefit estimates for each round of cost cutting described in this chapter.

ROUND 1: ACROSS-THE-BOARD COST CUTS

Spreadsheet for Calculating Cost Savings

Line	Item	Savings
1	Number of employees taking voluntary severance	[No. × Annual total compensation cost per employee]*
2	Number of employees taking early retirement	(No. × Annual total compensation cost per employee)*
3	Cut overtime	(% × Total annual salary cost)
4	Mandatory pay cut	(% × Total annual salary cost)
5	Perquisite reduction	(% × Total annual perquisite cost)
6	Reduced 401k contribution	(% × Total annual salary cost)
7	Reduced annual pay increases	(% × Total annual salary cost)
8	Reduced annual bonuses	(% × total annual salary cost)
9	Hiring freeze	[No. × Annual total compensation cost per employee per year]
10	Grand total annual savings	(Sum Lines 1–9)

*First year savings impacted by severance costs.

ROUND 2: ALTERNATIVE WORK ARRANGEMENTS

Spreadsheet for Calculating the Overall Net Cost Reduction of Alternative Work Arrangements

Line	Alternative	Definition	No. Employees	Total	Cost Reduction	Cost to Implement	Net Cost Reduction
1	Job/skill sharing	Reduce % salaries	No.	Total salaries	(% × Total)	Negligible	(Cost reduction − Cost to implement)
2	Contracting	Reduce 100% of total annual compensation cost	No.	Total compensation	(100%)	Total of contracting fees	(Cost reduction − Cost to implement)
3	Offsite Net workers	Reduce to % salaries	No.	Total salaries	(% × Total)	Start-up costs	(Cost reduction − Cost to implement)
4	Special projects	Reduce % salaries	No.	Total salaries	(% × Total)	Negligible	(Cost reduction − Cost to implement)
5	Overall Net Cost Reduction						(Sum Lines 1–4)

ROUND 3: LAYOFFS

Spreadsheet for Calculating the Net Short-Term Cost Savings (Benefit) of a Layoff

Line		Amount
	Long-Term Savings	
1	Annual total compensation cost per employee	(Annual total compensation cost/employee)
2	Total number of employees to be laid off	(No. of employees to be laid off)
3	Total Long-Term cost savings	(Annual total compensation cost/employee × No. to be laid off)
	Short-Term Cost to Implement	
4	Outplacement services (generally a minimum of $500 per employee)	($ in outplacement services per employee)
5	Severance package per employee (generally several weeks pay and benefit continuation for each year of service)	($ in salary and benefit continuation per employee)
6	Accumulated paid vacation	($ in accumulated vacation per employee)
7	Total cost per employee	(Sum Lines 4–6)
8	Total cost to implement layoff	(Multiply Line 2 × Line 7)
9	Net Short-Term Cost Savings (Benefit)	(Line 3 − Line 8)

• ROUND 3: LAYOFFS

Spreadsheet for Calculating the Real Long-Term Cost of a Layoff

Line	Item	Amount
1	Recruitment, selection, and orientation cost expended per employee laid off (can amount to $12,500 to screen and $7500 to orient)	($ per employee laid off)
2	Training investment per employee hired as a replacement (can amount to $3000 per person per year)	($ per employee laid off)
3	Recruitment, selection, and orientation cost expended per employee hired as a replacement (can amount to $12,500 to screen and $ 7500 to orient)	($ per employee laid off)
4	Market premium paid to attract replacement into the company	($ difference between salary of the laid-off person and salary offered to the replacement)
5	Cost of additional supervision (estimate the percentage of a supervisor's time required during the first year times the supervisor's salary)	(% of additional supervisor's time required × supervisor's salary)
6	Economic opportunity cost of lower productivity during first year of the replacement's employment	(% at which the new person works × estimate of the value of his work output during the first year)
7	Total long-term cost per replacement	(Sum Lines 1–6)
8	Number laid off	(No. laid off)
9	Total long-term cost for replacing those laid off	Line 7 × Line 8

Step 3: Decide Whom to Cut and Whom to Keep

KEY PRINCIPLES

- The key factor in determining whom to cut and whom to keep is mission critical skills and competencies.

- Mission critical skills and competencies must be defined for the organization as a whole and for each department.

- Employees should be assessed regarding mission critical skills and competencies.

- Once these skills and competencies are assessed, the company can make smart choices about which staff to cut and which to keep.

FROM ECONOMIC PLANNING TO ACTION

The way should now be clear to plan for the three rounds of cost cutting that comprise the headcount solution: (1) making across-the-board compensation cuts that can be accomplished without layoffs; (2) instituting alternatives to traditional full-time employment that will cut employment costs while retaining human capital; and (3) conducting layoffs only as a last ditch effort. This chapter focuses on one last difficult decision that needs to be made to translate this economic plan into action: deciding whom to cut and whom to keep.

At this point in a company's schedule, time is critical. Managers won't have a lot of time to reflect and gather facts. The steps that follow don't take long—perhaps one-half to one day of a department manager's attention. But the decision must be made methodically and acted upon swiftly. The worst thing to do at this juncture is to act scared and helpless like a deer caught in the headlights of a car. The key, instead, is to focus and spend time now rather than put off the hard choices for later.

A large amount of data and analysis is not necessary to make effective decisions about cutting and keeping people. Here's a blueprint of how to approach this task. Most information will be in employee files. Make sure the human resources staff can secure the following data for each employee, preferably in electronic form:

1. Name
2. Job assignment
3. Last three performance reviews if available
4. Current salary
5. Years with the department
6. Years with the company

Department managers should conduct this analysis of their departments. Why? Because it is necessary to act quickly, without a lot of time spent on lengthy group meetings and involvement. Second, confidentiality is critical. Tough decisions must be made about who will have the opportunity to move with the company into its new stage and who will have to find employment elsewhere.

Keep in mind the goal is to get the costs out while holding onto the talent needed to make the company thrive again. The choices made will translate cost-cutting economics into an action plan that identifies whom to cut and keep. The decision is best made in three steps:

Step 1 : Establish human capital priorities. List the skills and competencies that are most critical to a department's mission and core operations.

Step 2 : Determine the appropriate combination of alternative work arrangements and layoffs. This will help to identify the options such as job/skill sharing and temporary assignments that are feasible and can be quickly implemented.

Step 3 : Match people with employment choices. Make the final choices of who will be retained in full employment, who will be offered alternative work arrangements, and who will be asked to leave.

STEP 1: ESTABLISH HUMAN CAPITAL PRIORITIES

In the CWE/WorldatWork survey discussed in Chapter 2, the vast majority of respondents reported that preserving human capital was a major concern in conducting layoffs. Yet many times mass layoffs are conducted either through an across-the-board policy or one that attempts to lay off staff in reverse order of seniority. Both policies can be defended on the grounds of fairness or equity from an employee-relations perspective. However, they both come up woefully short when held up to a standard of business rationality.

A smarter approach is to first to consider the needs of the company when faced with the pressure to lay off staff. Specifically, managers should ask, "What's in the best interest of the business?" when considering options. In terms of human capital, the question boils down to, "Which employees have the mission-critical skills and where are they?"

The decision maker must determine quickly who is needed to fulfill the primary tasks of maintaining the organization and running the business. This does not mean creating wish lists or putting together generalities. Rather, it means that department managers should make some timely choices of who goes and who stays based on tough business priorities. Following is an example that's a compilation of how cuts are handled based on the experience of a number of businesses.

The department is an information technology (IT) unit that services a property and casualty insurance company. A mission has been undertaken to turn the company's poor financial performance around. The CEO has asked all unit managers (including IT) to come up with a plan for cutting salaries by 30 percent within the month. The department consists of 16 full-time employees and provides two kinds of services to the insurance company's line of business (LOB) organization: (1) providing new software installation, upgrading, and maintenance, and (2) supporting customer service primarily through troubleshooting problems as they develop.

The manager has already identified across-the-board costs to cut (discussed in Chapter 4). He knows how to cut roughly 5 percent of the 30 percent of the costs that must be removed. But he also knows that 25 percent more will have to come out later. Eliminating those costs will involve decisions about people. So he has reached the stage where he must choose those who will stay (either as full-time employees or part-time employees in some other work arrangement) and those whom he will have to fire.

The manager needs to take a few minutes to compile a list of strategic and process competencies for the IT department (as shown in Table 6-1). Strategic competencies define how a business will achieve and sustain a competitive advantage in its market. In this case, the insurance company has pursued two strategies: (1) a reputation for highly customized insurance products and (2) rapid, flawless customer service. These two strategic competencies are the basis for building competitive advantage. He needs to ask, "What strategic and process competencies does the IT department need to accomplish this strategy?" The answer is listed in Table 6-1.

Note, for example, that if the insurance company achieves and maintains a reputation for customized financial products and customer service, it will need state-of-the-art information technology from the IT department. It will also need an immediate response from IT when troubles crop up or systems go down.

Two major processes contribute to support the company's strategy. The first is state-of-the-art technology. IT must assure that all information systems (hardware and software) are current. That requires continuous research and upgrading of systems.

Table 6-1   Strategic and Process Competencies

Level		Competency
Company strategy	Key to competitive advantage	Reputation for customized financial products Customer service
IT department process	Key to supporting competitive advantage IT department competencies: What people do	State-of-the-art technology Internal customer service
		Software languages Operating systems Hardware systems Databases Applications Network administration Project management

The second process is customer service. The insurance company will require that IT deliver flawless customer service. It will need to deliver uninterrupted high-quality service to keep systems up and running and to troubleshoot and bring systems back quickly to top working order.

The manager must define process competencies first and then define the critical activities required to accomplish the department's objectives. Taking matters a step further, managers should ask, "What will it take on behalf of our people to assure state-of-the-art technology and rapid customer service to the LOB internal clients (e.g., insurance operations and policy service)?" To answer this question, managers need to determine what competencies are demanded in terms of the skills people actually need and find out who has them. The answer is in the lower right side of Table 6-1:

1. Software languages: Proficiency in basic languages to develop software.

2. Operating systems: Proficiency in customer operating systems.

3. Hardware systems: Proficiency in customer platforms.

4. Databases: Proficiency in databases to support applications.

5. Applications: Proficiency on customer-driven applications.

6. Network administration: Proficiency in developing and maintaining systems on the network.

7. Project management: Proficiency to manage project teams.

Staff will have to be proficient in software systems and operating languages. They will need hardware and database skills. They will have to know how to manage networks flawlessly. And they will need to be capable project managers, which means that they will have to know how to bring in tasks on budget, with quality results achieved on time.

Once process competencies have been identified, managers must use them to assess employees in the department in order to find people who most closely meet them. These are the people most critical to the mission and who will be considered foremost for retention when cost-cutting decisions are made.

By examining the department's processes closely, the manager forces herself to address what goes on in the IT department and what people actually do. This discipline helps to establish the priorities, which become the business-related basis for making choices about who goes and stays.

The next task is to determine who in the department has these process competencies and how they can best be employed, given the costs that have to be removed. The analysis in this step will prepare managers to decide who will stay as full-time employees, who will be allocated to an alternative work arrangement, and who will be laid off.

Note how different this procedure is compared to traditional layoffs. In contrast to the traditional practice, this approach places business needs as the primary consideration and employee considerations as a support driver. Be careful. The primary question is not, "Who has been most faithful?" or "Who is the best individual performer?" but "Who is most critical to the core business?" followed by, "Who are the best performers with respect to the core business?"

Here's the rub, however. Some will ask, "Doesn't loyalty count for something or anything any longer?" Yes, but managers will have a conflict if they keep people based on their time with the organization. Managers face important choices. They can keep people who are loyal, long-term employees, but these are not necessarily the ones most capable of turning around the business. Or they can choose the players who have the greatest chance to turn the company around irrespective of past service.

Here's another key question, "Doesn't merit count anymore?" Yes, but it is not sufficient. Again, it will not help the company to retain its best performers if those with a previous history of good performance do not happen to have the skills needed to survive and thrive in the future.

In reality this is not a clean or easy decision. In fact, the best managers must balance all the considerations of who is most skilled, who puts forth the extra effort, and who are the most committed, long-term contributors. Achieving the right balance among these criteria requires a prioritization that goes something like this:

- First, who has the skills needed to maintain the mission and core operations?
- Second, within this group, who are the best performers?
- In the same group, who are the long-term contributors?

The answer to these questions will yield the people who should be kept first and foremost.

Making the decision of whom to keep, cut, and assign to alternative work arrangements requires weighing many different criteria and applying judgment and wisdom. The judgment and wisdom surface most importantly when dealing with loyal, long-term employees who do not have the skills to lead the company into the future.

In a period of low unemployment and numerous job opportunities, an ample severance package will support a laid-off employee for a reasonable time during a job search. Even in good economic times, however, the stress that comes with having to terminate an employee coupled with the onus of knowing the shame and loss of self-esteem often disturbs managers so much that they will try to avoid a serious human capital assessment. Instead, they adopt rules of thumb to side-step such judgments. For example, the "last-in, first-out" approach basically gets managers off the hook from making tough decisions about skills and performance levels.

In addition fair employment practice rules and regulations must be factored into these decisions. Companies need to consider the risk of costly violations of fair employment practice laws (e.g., Title VII of the Civil Rights Act, Age Discrimination in Employment Act, WARN, etc., which will be covered in Chapter 9).

The following six guidelines for human capital decision making will greatly increase opportunities for success:

1. **Employ decision-making criteria that are defensible and based on business relatedness.** Skills and competencies that are related to executing strategies are clearly business related and defensible on their face. The same is true for decisions based on job or task performance. However, the whole area of personal characteristics and traits such as energy, drive, and attitude is troublesome and subjective. Judging differences between people on these types of criteria is hard to document, defend, and explain. It makes more sense to stick to the most objective criteria possible, which involve issues directly related to business success. For example, specify skills in terms of on-the-job work performed or successful completion of job-related tests of skills. Or use performance ratings that are based on job-related work.

2. **Communicate the plan for the human capital analysis to all employees.** This period of time is incredibly stressful. Managers are reluctant to talk about the process because they probably do not know how it will end up—who will stay and who will go. Consequently, everyone is tight lipped. It is possible to communicate the process without dealing with the results that are to come on an individual level, and that is exactly what should be done. This should include steps and timetables. This approach will actually be a boon to managers because it will take some of the pressure off them and provide a frame of reference for questions posed.

3. **Educate managers on the tasks ahead and the pitfalls to avoid.** Along with communication to all employees, special background information should be provided to managers. Subjects should include:

   - The process the company is going through and how to manage it.
   - Tips for coaching and counseling.

- How to get assistance in dealing with distraught employees (if necessary).

- How to conduct the headcount analysis.

This background material can be communicated either in written form or in up-front training or coaching.

4. **Ensure that personal biases do not enter into human capital decisions.** A company manager may be unconsciously biased toward one employee or another. This may be due to personal likes (or dislikes) that are the result of previous social encounters. Bias can also be the result of stereotypes people have based on personal beliefs and lack of knowledge. That's why it's important to stick to judgments based solely on criteria relevant to the job and the company and not on personal biases. Managers must essentially erase such potential biases from the task at hand when making human capital decisions to ensure future company success.

5. **Develop a complete profile on each employee and use the same criteria for assessing all employees.** To be totally consistent, each employee should be reviewed in exactly the same way using the same criteria. Additionally, complete documentation should be collected for every employee. The best defense for any claims of unfair treatment is demonstration of a thorough and completely documented analysis based on business-related criteria.

6. **Take a "snapshot" of the employee base before and after you make human capital decisions. Compare the work force differences as a check on your decisions.** When the manager is done with the analysis, he or she should take a before-and-after look at the decisions that have been made. Is there a pattern of bias against any particular EEO protected group? Is there an implication of favoritism? Would an outsider question these decisions on a common sense basis? If the answer is "yes," then the manager should make sure that the treatment of employees can be defended on business-related criteria.

STEP 2: DETERMINE THE COMBINATION OF ALTERNATIVE WORK ARRANGEMENTS AND LAYOFFS THAT WILL BEST HELP THE COMPANY

The second step in deciding whom to cut and keep is to determine what alternative work arrangements are practical, in conjunction with layoffs, to result in the needed cost reductions and retention of human capital. What is feasible for an organization will depend on its needs and flexibility in human resources policies (e.g., employment, compensation, and benefits). One thing is for sure. The earlier the managers start the process, the greater the flexibility and number of options they have at their disposal.

Notwithstanding the constraints, Table 6-2 identifies each of the alternative work arrangements to be considered and discusses the best fit scenario for each. As each alternative in the table is considered, managers need to ask if each is feasible: "Am I free to implement this without seeking a lot of permission?" Second, they need to ask if they have the resources to implement it quickly. The start-up cost and time involved are other questions. Offsite Net workers might require the company investing in information technology (laptops, modems, and networking software such as virtual private networks), which costs several thousand dollars per head. In addition, such an option will require training both for supervisors and employees in how to use and manage the technology as well as supervision while working from home and away from readily available support desk help.

Finally, there is the matter of time. An important cost savings associated with this option is reduced real expense. This can be achieved by paring floor space. With fewer people at work, less space is needed. Most department heads won't have immediate control over this variable. They may be locked into a multiyear lease, and corporate officers may be the ones designated to decide about space options.

The IT manager needs to examine these options even further. First, he rules out offsite Net workers. This idea isn't feasible, given the need

Table 6-2　Alternative Work Arrangements

Alternative	Best Fit Scenario
Job/skill sharing	Work can be shared without losing accountability for results. Collaboration and sharing are core cultural values. Incumbents have superior team and interpersonal skills.
Contracting arrangements	Job function is self-contained and relatively independent. Job function includes highly specialized knowledge and skill sets. Incumbents have the skill and discipline to work without close supervision.
Offsite Net workers	Advanced telecommunication technology is available. Work can be accomplished independently with little need for coordination. Incumbents have the skill and discipline to work without close supervision.
Temporary assignments	Projects have definite scope with a beginning and an end. Projects of high priority require immediate attention. Incumbents can adapt well to deadlines and frequent changes in assignments.

to move quickly. Job/skill sharing will work better. The department has a number of people who may be interested in maintaining employment but at a reduced time level. Some are working spouses interested in freeing up time for family. Several others are close to retirement and would like to ease off from a full-time workload. The manager also needs to find people who are willing to accept part-time work. He needs to find people, however, who can work as a team and understand that job sharing means sharing accountability for deadlines and performance.

Next the manager needs to consider contracting arrangements in which an employee ceases to be an employee and comes to work as an outside contractor. Although this appears attractive, it is a solution fraught with potential legal problems. If the employee is neither truly working independently nor supplying his or her own tools, the company might be found liable for violating Internal Revenue Service regulations and employment laws. The manager decides to pass on this option, at least for now.

Temporary assignments are the last alternative option to consider in Table 6-2. Some of the work in the IT department reflects a project nature rather than ongoing work. Software modification and upgrading occur when needed (e.g., for a new product installation).

This is not a continuing process in the IT department. Note that some systems analysts and network analysis positions might be well adapted to temporary assignments rather than to full-time employment. Whoever is chosen for special assignments, however, should be a self-starter and skilled at managing projects to meet deadlines.

The foregoing analysis concludes with the manager's choice among the four options for deciding who goes and who stays:

1. Retain the person as a full-time employee
2. Job share
3. Special assignment
4. Layoff

STEP 3: MATCH PEOPLE WITH EMPLOYMENT CHOICES AND MOVE ON

The final step is to match every employee in the department with one of the four employment options. In considering this analysis, managers must begin with two quick checks. First, they must consider the transaction cost associated with each option listed in Table 6-3. Note that only the layoff has a significant transaction cost associated with it. (See Chapter 5.) In this case it has been estimated that it will cost 25 percent of an employee's annual salary to lay that person off (based on real case studies). The figure includes separation costs such as outplacement services, accrued vacation, and severance packages. Costs associated with the other options will be nil.

Table 6-3   First-Year Transaction Cost

Action	Transaction Cost (as a Percentage of Salary)
Layoff	25%
Job share	0%
Special assignment	0%
Retain as regular employee	0%

Table 6-4   First-Year Net Savings

Action	Gross Savings	Transaction Cost	Net Cost Savings
Layoff	100%	25%	75%
Job share	50%	0%	50%
Special assignment	30%	0%	30%
Retain as regular employee	0%	0%	0%

Next a table should be prepared for expressing the net cost savings for each action (Table 6-4). The layoff option, for example, will result in gross savings of 100 percent of an employee's current salary. The net cost savings will be the gross savings of 100 percent less the transaction cost of 25 percent, or 75 percent.

The IT manager is now ready to begin an employee-by-employee analysis as appears in Table 6-5.

The following information will be needed for each employee:

- Job title gives the job assignment, the role the person is playing in the IT department.

- Time in the department and time in the company provide information on longevity or tenure (something that is not of prime consideration but still may be of some importance to the manager in making choices).

- Last three performance ratings—indicate the past performance effectiveness of the employee.

- Current pay is the employee's current annual salary rate.

- Technical skills rating — There are seven ratings that must go into the manager's judgments (see Table 6-1):
  1. Software languages: Proficiency in basic languages to develop software.
  2. Operating systems: Proficiency in customer operating systems.
  3. Hardware systems: Proficiency in customer platforms.

Table 6-5 Spreadsheet for Employee Analysis

Information Technology Department

Employee Name	Job Title	Time in Dept.	Time in Co.	Last 3 Perf. Rtgs.	Technical Skills Rating							Tot Pts.	Current Pay*
					1	2	3	4	5	6	7		
M. Burr	Sr. Systems Analyst	4	10	3-3-3	3	3	4	3	4	3	3	23	$44,000
E. Larty	Sr. Systems Analyst	4	6	3-4-3	5	2	4	2	4	3	5	25	$43,000
R. Boyd	Systems Analyst	2	6	4-4-4	4	3	4	4	5	4	4	28	$38,600
S. Bruno	Systems Analyst	1	3	4-5-4	3	3	4	3	4	3	3	23	$35,300
D. Evtag	Systems Analyst	1	3	5-4-3	3	3	3	2	2	2	2	17	$39,300
C. Johns	Systems Analyst	1	1	5	5	4	4	4	5	5	5	32	$36,200
M. Morco	Systems Analyst	2	4	2-4-3	2	2	3	2	3	2	3	17	$32,500
D. Trever	Systems Analyst	1	1	3	2	2	3	2	3	2	2	16	$37,100
G. Wang	Sr. Network Analyst	5	8	5-5-4	4	5	5	5	4	5	5	33	$55,000
B. Turco	Network Analyst	2	2	3-3	3	2	4	2	5	3	3	22	$45,200
M. Fontaine	Sr. Customer Support Spec.	9	18	3-3-3	4	3	4	3	3	3	2	22	$34,700
B. Hungo	Customer Support Spec.	10	15	3-3-3	3	3	2	2	3	3	2	18	$34,500
M. Moroney	Customer Support Spec.	ˋ8	12	4-4-4	4	5	4	4	3	4	4	28	$28,600
G. Sartee	Customer Support Spec.	6	6	4-4-4	4	5	4	4	3	4	4	28	$30,200
F. Truncheon	Customer Support Spec.	6	6	3-2-3	2	2	3	2	3	3	2	17	$27,100
R. Younger	Customer Support Spec.	1	1	5	4	3	4	4	2	4	2	23	$31,000
													$592,300

*Only salary costs are considered in this example.

4. Databases: Proficiency in databases to support applications.

5. Applications: Proficiency in customer-driven applications (e.g., business development, policy issue, claims).

6. Network administration: Proficiency in developing and maintaining systems on network platforms.

7. Project management: Capability to manage project teams.

Assessments on these seven criteria are probably the only information that cannot be supplied to the manager making the assessment. Managers may, as a result, have to make this assessment on their own. To do so, consider the following:

Step 1: Develop a five-point scale to assess an employee's level on each skill, for example:

Unqualified	Partly Qualified	Qualified	Highly Qualified	Expert
1	2	3	4	5
☐	☐	☐	☐	☐

Step 2: Be careful to develop detailed descriptions of unqualified, partly qualified, qualified, highly qualified, and expert for each skill area.

Step 3: Rate each employee on each of the seven skill areas. The result will be a technical skill rating for each employee on each skill. Enter the data in the spreadsheet.

Step 4: Calculate the total points earned in the technical skills rating for each employee. The result will be an overall technical skill rating for each employee.

The overall technical skill rating will be especially important because the manager will want to make sure that those employees who will best embody the seven competencies critical to IT's processes will be identified. They are absolutely essential to the IT department's functioning and, ultimately, contribution to the insurance company's mission and survival. These calculations should take no more than a few hours for the 16 people in the example.

Putting yourself in the position of the IT manager, get ready to use the spreadsheet in Table 6-5 to make the choices. It may take two or more rounds to reach the goal. Balance concerns of skill level, performance, and time either in the department or in the company. It's important to find a placement among the four options (retain, job share, temporary assignment, lay off) that will enable the firm to reduce 25 percent of its employment costs while keeping those most critical to the operation. Prioritize criteria as described earlier in this chapter: First, do a skill rating; second, conduct a performance rating; third and last, consider time in the department or company.

The results of the first pass are presented in Table 6-6. First, it is decided that that Boyd and Bruno are both systems analysts with some experience and excellent performance ratings. Most managers wouldn't want to lose either. They both have the competencies needed. Perhaps they will both be amenable to share the job, at least for several months, until the business turns around. Make note again that this option will only work if they are willing to accept the notion and work together.

Moving on, the managers note that Evtag has little experience in the department and his competence ratings aren't that high. In addition, Morco, Turco, and Truncheon have relatively low performance ratings and do not have high scores with respect to the competencies needed. Those four are probably the best candidates for layoffs. Finally Fontane and Younger are candidates to job share.

It now can be calculated how much will be saved if the plan in Table 6-6 is executed. Salary costs are cut 30 percent. Moreover, this is a conservative figure because benefits costs saved by the layoff have not been factored in. To make the forecast even more accurate, managers may want to bulk up the salary savings by 30 to 40 percent

Table 6-6   First-Round Analysis

Employee	Action	Salary	Factor	Net Savings
D. Evtag	Layoff	$39,300	75%	$29,475
R. Boyd	Job share	$38,600	50%	$19,300
S. Bruno	Job share	$35,300	50%	$17,650
M. Morco	Layoff	$32,500	75%	$24,375
B. Turco	Layoff	$45,200	75%	$33,900
F. Truncheon	Layoff	$27,100	75%	$20,325
M. Fontaine	Job share	$34,700	50%	$17,350
R. Younger	Job Share	$31,000	50%	$15,500
Total savings				$177,875
As percentage of budget				30%

(the additional cost of benefits) in their calculations for those who are laid off.

The 30 percent savings exceeds the 25 percent that had to be cut. So smart managers go to a second round of analysis to retain more human capital and still get the 25 percent of compensation costs out.

Some other changes should be considered. Instead of laying off Turco, he might be able to be put on a special assignment. He's the only network analyst in the department (other than G. Wang). Putting him on assignment retains those skills. In addition, M. Fontaine and R. Younger seem more critical to retain. Rather than sharing a job and going down to half time, the managers try to find special assignments for them that will allow both to stay employed at a 70 percent level. This second strategy is considered and the resulting cost savings appear in Table 6-7.

The analysis is now complete. There is a way to get 25 percent of the cost out of the unit while maximizing the retention of valued human capital.

The last task for the managers is to confer with each employee so that the layoffs and transition to any new roles run as smoothly as possible. Finally, it is time for everyone to move on into their new roles.

Table 6-7   Second-Round Analysis

Name	Action	Salary	Factor	Net Savings
D. Evtag	Layoff	$39,300	75%	$29,475
R. Boyd	Job share	$38,600	50%	$19,300
S. Bruno	Job share	$35,300	50%	$17,650
M. Morco	Layoff	$32,500	75%	$24,375
B. Turco	Special assignment	$45,200	30%	$13,560
F. Truncheon	Layoff	$27,100	75%	$20,325
M. Fontaine	Special assignment	$34,700	30%	$10,410
R. Younger	Special assignment	$31,000	30%	$9,300
Total savings				$144,395
As percentage of budget				24.4%

GUIDELINES TO MATCH PEOPLE WITH ALTERNATIVE WORK ARRANGEMENTS

However it is accomplished, the matching process must be completed quickly and in a fashion that meets the company's standards of internal and external fairness. Following are guidelines for accomplishing this process:

1. It is important to determine the interests of employees in the various options available. Polling people on what they think of the alternatives can accomplish this.

2. Reassignments should be applied at the department or work group level, especially if job/skill sharing is considered. Temporary assignments, however, can cross departmental lines.

3. In making the assignments to employees, resources for management support must be taken into account. Without such support, offsite Net workers will not be effective in their roles.

There are several practical issues to consider regarding the decision of whom to cut and keep. First, the example presented here involves department managers as sole decision makers. As we recommended, this will keep decisions close to the work group and can be done quickly. However, in many large, complex organizations, it may be necessary to coordinate decision making through a task force of fellow managers that is overseen by corporate officers and even the CEO.

A second concern regards employee choices: What are their interests? Many employees wonder, "Don't we get a choice in this case?" In a strict sense the answer is "no." The purpose of the exercise discussed previously is to save the company money, not to provide maximum choice to employees. What can be done is to let people know ahead of time what managers are considering and poll employees' interests. Ideally, their interests can be accommodated as long as the cost reduction and human capital goals are still met. In so doing managers allow individuals to make choices where possible.

What's the right thing to do? Managers must be the ones to conduct the analysis and make decisions quickly. These decisions must be communicated openly and swiftly. Finally, they must allow employees to make choices available to them.

What if employees don't accept options open to them? As previously stressed, the objective is to balance the company's strategic requirements with employee needs. Because time is of the essence, employees should be given a reasonable but limited window of opportunity to provide their input, and then everyone must move forward.

EXECUTING THE HEADCOUNT SOLUTION

This chapter and Chapter 5 describe the planning that managers must do to prepare for the headcount solution. The next four chapters will show how to execute the headcount solution. Chapter 7 will describe in practical terms those steps to take to get the first round of costs out. Chapter 8 will show how to deploy alternative work arrangements and get people into them. Chapter 9 will show how to conduct a layoff in a way that is efficient, respectful, dignified, and defensible. Chapter 10 will explain how to help survivors get back to business.

SUMMARY

- Acting wisely requires planning ahead: (1) establish human capital priorities; (2) determine the combination of nonlayoff cost cuts, alternative work arrangements, and layoffs that will work best for the department and company; (3) match people with new work arrangements; and (4) move on to Step 4 of the headcount solution.

- Taking the time to conduct a human capital needs assessment before laying off staff will pay off by allowing managers to retain the skills and competencies needed for the business rebound that lies ahead.

CHAPTER 7

Step 4: Implement Across-The-Board Cuts

KEY PRINCIPLES

- The first round of cost cutting should be aimed at broad-based employee groups rather than at specific individuals.

- Voluntary severance and retirement options should be carefully considered before moving ahead. They are legally complex and could lead to losing valuable human capital.

- Senior leadership should consider numerous alternatives before proceeding and balance costs that can be saved against the potential for disruptive impact.

- Companies can successfully involve employees in developing suggestions for the first round of cost cutting.

THE FIRST ROUND OF COMPENSATION COST CUTTING

When facing a need to reduce operating costs, the first round of compensation cost cutting should concentrate on areas that impact broad groups of employees rather than target specific staff. They should not include involuntary separations or layoffs. There are many ways to cut costs before instituting layoffs. Layoffs are disruptive and require collecting information and analysis regarding employee skills and job performance that may not be available at the beginning of a business crisis. It's likely additional cuts that will include alternative work arrangements and layoffs will follow the first round of cost cuts. These take time to implement.

This chapter provides details on 10 cost-cutting measures that companies can employ. But first there are some success stories.

COMPANIES THAT HAVE SUCCESSFULLY EMPLOYED ACROSS-THE-BOARD CUTS IN COMPENSATION COSTS

Following are stories from two companies that cut costs to avoid as many layoffs as possible. A West Coast medical center received its cue from the top when it came to cost reductions. The CEO set the stage. If an employee earned $100,000, he or she could volunteer to defer for cash flow purposes 20 percent of each paycheck to go into a fund to be paid in the future. The director of administration said the strategy was close to her heart. Employees were told the company was in a slump and preparing for a long-term contract to end, so it asked for volunteers. It seemed worth it to many to keep their jobs. The employees didn't lose anything; they only postponed being paid some cash. The strategy worked well except for employees who had grown accustomed to living on every cent of their paycheck. Having a lump sum coming to some employees in the future was very appealing.

Here's an example of another company strategy to avoid layoffs. World Now is a provider of Internet technology and revenue solutions for media companies. Jennifer Edwards, director of human resources, said that her firm asked employees for cost-cutting ideas. Managment felt that engaging employees in the decision-making process would result in changes with greater buy-in across the board. Edwards noted that senior leadership went to the employees and said, "This is your company. You're the owners and stockholders, and we want your input. We aren't telling you what to do. We want you to tell us." The company launched a project where each team of employees went offsite and did a brain blast. The teams worked to develop ideas either to generate more revenue or to reduce costs. Initial ideas were then handed off to those who could best research them. The suggestions were sent back to management in the form of 65 or 70 new ideas, details on how to implement them, and the potential revenue and savings. Everyone participated in this exercise, from the CEO down to the mailroom staffers.

The ideas were pared to 30 and then whittled down to the best 15, which were put in place immediately. For example, the company had been outsourcing projects such as printing collateral materials. Because the firm designs Web sites, staff reasoned, why not leverage the in-house creative team and manage the process internally? Additionally, they discovered that purchasing was conducted by many different people in different places. As a result of this exercise, purchasing was consolidated and relocated, and one employee known as a "ferocious negotiator" was assigned to handle the task, leveraging internal talent and saving substantial dollars. The company also eliminated daily catered lunches. Finally, saving were shaved from offsite team-building retreats. Rather than spend $30,000 on such meetings, the company found less expensive, creative ways to get everyone together. It was important for the company to maintain its culture, and it did so, but on a different, less expensive scale.

The theme at these companies and others was to get employees involved in cost cutting. Such strategies generate interest and motivation in a very positive way. Employees are likely to support the measures taken because they were involved in developing the ideas. However, in subsequent rounds of cost cutting that involve changing job assignments and involuntarily separations, employee involvement is not recommended. The reason is that it may place fellow employees in the inappropriate position of recommending one another for a pay reduction or terminated employment.

WHAT ARE ACROSS-THE-BOARD COST-CUTTING MEASURES?

The cost-cutting strategies that are a part of the first-round cuts outlined here are called *across-the-board cuts*. Cost cutting based on alternative work arrangements (the second round of cost cutting) and layoffs (the third round of cost cutting) are not across-the-board because they are targeted at individual employees based on how they perform skills at work. This first round deals with voluntary separations based on employee choice and other means of cutting compensation costs.

Across-the-board refers to approaches that do not attempt to single out employees for special treatment or termination. The costs saved in the first round rarely meet the overall cost reduction requirement, and additional rounds are needed.

WHY IMPLEMENT ACROSS-THE-BOARD COST-CUTTING MEASURES FIRST?

The first round of cuts involves voluntary separations and cost reductions that spread the pain across the employee population. These cuts may disappoint, but they do not cause the same negative consequences that layoffs do. In effect it is wise to condition the work force to the seriousness of the situation and the difficult decisions that senior leadership may need to make down the road.

10 ACROSS-THE-BOARD COST-CUTTING MEASURES

The 10 approaches that should be considered are:

1. **Voluntary severance incentive.** Offer an incentive to employees to leave the company voluntarily. Many may have considered the idea but resisted for lack of a push and funds.

2. **Early retirement incentive.** Offer an incentive to employees close to retirement age to take an "early out" that accelerates benefits related to retirement. Again, many may have thought about doing this but need a push or extra funds to take the step.

3. **Shorter work week.** Reduce hours to be worked during the work week and reduce base pay.

4. **Mandatory pay cut.** Require everyone to take an across-the-board cut in pay, including top management and even the CEO, president, or founder.

5. **Stock options in lieu of pay.** Grant employees stock options instead of some part of their current pay or in place of a pay increase. Although not as popular as they were a few years back, stock options can offer an incentive to remain in a company especially if a rebound at the company and in the overall economy is expected. If the company expects to make a public offering down the road, this becomes even more of an incentive.

6. **Reduction of perquisites.** Cut out company cars, expense accounts, subsidized lunches, golf club memberships, retreats, travel, and so forth. Few will miss these perks and those who do will learn to accept the change when it is presented for the right reasons.

7. **Reduction or elimination of 401(k) contribution.** Reduce the dollar contribution and/or match to qualified retirement plans.

8. **Reduction or suspension of annual pay increases.** Cancel all or part of planned merit pay or across-the-board pay increases.

9. **Reduction or suspension of bonuses and incentives.** Cancel all or part of planned bonuses and incentive payments. Replace them with bonuses contingent on turning around the business.

10. **Hiring freeze.** Suspend hiring new people for the foreseeable future, but let out the word that good people are always welcome to apply. Make it clear that when the company's situation improves, applicants will be considered.

VOLUNTARY SEVERANCE INCENTIVE

Voluntary severance is an incentive to leave the company on one's own volition. A severance package can be offered to all employees or to a segment of the labor force. For example, it can be targeted at employees in the factory, at a call center, or in administrative headquarters. It can also be targeted at hourly or salaried employees. Although the company can govern the group that voluntary severance is offered to, it should not discourage an individual eligible for a voluntary severance package from accepting it once he or she has opted to take it. If so, the company may risk litigation under federal laws and regulations.

Severance packages vary in what they offer. In general, severance pay includes a formula for one or more weeks pay for each year of service. At higher levels of the company, more generous offerings are made. The package may include accrued vacation pay, outplacement services, and other benefits.

The main benefit of a voluntary severance program is that it reduces work force costs without directly asking anyone to leave. It is less disruptive than a layoff.

The major ramifications of voluntary severance involve the lack of control over people who leave and the direct costs involved. Of course, once offered, anyone can accept a voluntary package. In effect the company may lose some of its good people and the important skills it needs to recover and grow in the future. This can be minimized if the program is properly targeted. The expenses incurred may also be a problem regarding current cashflow. As shown in Chapter 5, a careful analysis of the economics of short- versus long-term costs should be reviewed before considering a voluntary severance program. The shorter the period of crisis and turnaround that is anticipated, the less likely employees are to adopt this type of incentive.

The legal and regulatory issues regarding voluntary severance programs are complex, and it is quite important to comply with them. The consequences of noncompliance are severe.[1] Important issues include the following.

Employee Retirement Income Security Act (ERISA). Formal written severance policies may be subject to the reporting and disclosure requirements of ERISA. As such, severance would be treated as are other company benefits. Companies must carefully structure and communicate policies related to severance incentives and whether they should report the program to the government annually and comply with specific procedures for administration.

Older Workers' Benefit Protection Act (OWBPA). A voluntary severance incentive cannot be used as a means to discriminate against older workers or negatively affect other benefits that might be forthcoming to those eligible for retirement. In addition the company must comply with provisions of the Age Discrimination in Employment Act (ADEA). The OBPWA specifies regulations and rules for protection of employees who may be offered a number of benefits related to their

1. For more detail on this subject, refer to SHRM White Papers, "Severance Pay" by Terry L. Baglieri; "A Brief Overview of the Older Workers Benefit Protection' Act"; "New EEOC Guidance on Discrimination in Employee Benefits" by Timothy S. Bland; and "What Is an Employee to Do: Employment Termination, Severance and Waivers" by Frank A. Tola and Christopher K. Ramsey, Alexandria, VA: Society for Human Resource & Management.

employment termination. The act also specifies conditions under which employers may require waivers of future claims of discrimination. It is important to secure waivers to avoid future individual and/or class action litigation. (See Appendix A for a sample separation agreement.)

EARLY RETIREMENT INCENTIVE

Early retirement incentives are similar to severance incentives in that the company offers an enhanced package of additional benefits to leave active employment at the company. The enhanced package usually involves acceleration of pension benefits that are tied to years of service, level of pay, or both. By changing the benefit formula, retirement becomes a more attractive alternative. As with voluntary severance, the company can offer the incentive but cannot in any way coerce employees to stay or leave. A key difference between the early retirement incentive and voluntary severance incentive is that the population attracted to it is typically more tenured and older.

Employers can target this retirement incentive, but in a different way from voluntary severance. Targets can be set with regard to age and years of service that relate to the plan's design and benefit formulas.

The severance costs for early retirement incentives are borne by the pension plan and do not come directly from current revenue. This program, therefore, is less expensive in terms of the income statement or one-time capital costs than what's involved in a voluntary severance plan. Because the program is voluntary, it is much less disruptive than involuntary layoffs. Again, the downside is that management cannot control who stays and leaves. Therefore, the company may lose some of its critical human capital.

As with voluntary severance plans, the legal issues are complex and critical to consider before leaders act. The OWBPA governs conditions for requiring employees to sign waivers. There are also important considerations regarding the ADEA and Title VII of the Civil Rights Act.

Finally, the company must consider the potential conflict between incentives for early retirement as opposed to incentives for voluntary separation. If the company offers both plans, there may be some important legal considerations regarding potential discrimination.

SHORTER WORK WEEK

Typical work weeks in the United States are 40 hours or fewer. All employees are paid either by the hour or by a predetermined salary. If paid by the hour, employees are subject to the overtime provision and the Fair Labor Standards Act (FLSA) and state laws, if applicable. Accordingly, if the hourly employee works more than 40 hours in a given week, in most cases the employer must pay 150 percent of the base wage for every hour worked over the first 40 hours in the week.

Some salaried workers may also be subject to the overtime provisions of the FLSA based on the content of the job. If they are, the company is required to pay 150 percent, as it does for hourly workers, but this is subject to specific requirements of the law on a job-by-job basis. Some employers voluntarily pay overtime to salaried workers, especially if they work alongside the hourly workers when overtime is required. Most important, regardless of job title or pay level in the company, any employee who is paid by the hour is subject to the FLSA overtime requirements.

It is clear that the ripest of the "low-hanging fruit" (e.g., the first place to cut), which managers pick for cost cutting, is elimination of overtime as a company policy for a period of time to get through the business crisis. In addition, the company can reduce hours for a shorter work week by cutting the number of hours per day or cutting part of a day, such as a Friday afternoon.

For hourly employees, cutting the number of hours below 40 is automatically self-correcting because pay is based on the actual number of hours worked. For salaried employees, the situation is more complicated. By reducing the hours of salaried employees, the company may inadvertently change the status of salaried workers to that of hourly workers. So any hours over 40 worked by the salaried workers in this circumstance could generate an overtime premium for them. This is another case where the complications of legal compliance may make it too difficult to implement a cost-cutting measure.

A shorter work week raises morale issues regarding the amount of work required by employees. In a plant or factory, reducing the number of hours fits with reduced operations. In an administrative situation, the level of work required is not as identifiable. Senior leadership and management must clarify workloads and expected levels of effort to manage effectively throughout the crisis.

Overall, cutting hours back to 40 hours a week is a prime cost-cutting measure. Cutting hours below 40 is also a good cost-cutting strategy for hourly employees and salaried employees who are "not exempt" from overtime premiums of the FLSA. Cutting hours back for other salaried workers may not be a reasonable cost-cutting approach.

MANDATORY PAY CUT

A mandatory pay cut applies to base wages or salaries. It slashes pay without cutting back work required and without consideration of individual performance or skill. In effect it says to employees, "You will receive less money for doing the same thing because we do not have the ability to pay you your complete salary at the present time."

This approach differs from a shorter work week. With a shorter work week, fewer hours are worked and less work gets done. Presumably, there is less work to do because of a fall-off in volume, customers, and clients. A mandatory pay cut requires the same amount of work as before and may be perceived as unfair or inequitable. However, most employees perceive it as better than losing a job.

There are some important issues for senior leadership to consider in contemplating a mandatory pay cut.

Pay Competitiveness. When the company recovers, it will face a fall-off in the overall competitiveness of the pay package and will have to adjust pay upward. In the future, there will be the opportunity to increase pay rates selectively based on individual skill and performance.

Deferrals. Pay cuts can be handled as a deferral with a clear commitment to repay the deferral at a specific time in the future. (See earlier example.) The impact on morale may be dampened if the pay cut is handled as a deferral; however, employers should not make weak promises to repay in the future when employees look for strong leadership and stability about the future of the company.

Morale. Across-the-board pay cuts demoralize because of dashed expectations or, just as important, because of the impact on the employees' financial commitments such as mortgage or car payments. A pay cut may force individuals possessing critical human capital to consider alternative employment, and it invites headhunters to cherry-pick the best employees. However, a mandatory pay cut does not include reduced employee benefits. As long as a benefits package is not cut, people are less likely to leave in the short run.

To minimize morale from slumping, a turnaround incentive program like the kind described in Chapter 3 should accompany a mandatory pay cut. This will provide hope and a reason to remain with the company through the crisis.

STOCK OPTIONS IN LIEU OF PAY

Some publicly traded companies have provided stock options to supplement or replace part of base pay when cashflow decreases. This type of cost-cutting measure and incentive is used more typically in emerging entrepreneurial companies, especially in telecommunications and information technology.

A company cannot provide stock options as a supplement to pay below competitive levels for a very long time. Continuing to pay below competitive levels over several years will reduce the company's ability to retain talent. Employees with critical skills will eventually seek employment elsewhere. However, if the stock options accrue in value, they may become a retention tool. Eventually, as the company recovers from the crisis, base pay should return to competitive levels.

Stock options do not have the same intrinsic value to all employees because they represent the accrual of value over a period of years. If the paycheck represents an employee's primary means to meet basic needs, he or she will be less interested in being compensated tomorrow rather than today.

REDUCTION OF PERQUISITES

Perquisites are benefits provided to employee groups or individual employees, that have value to the employee and are work related. Perquisites range from subsidized meals to club memberships and expense accounts. In some cases the perquisites are taxable to the employee. Following are perquisites that companies should consider for the first round of cost cutting:

- **Automobile lease or cost reimbursement.** Automobile cost reimbursement can be cut back to only those employees who need autos for work on a daily basis.
- **Club memberships.** Club memberships, often provided to a broad group of managers and executives, can be cut back or eliminated, except for meals taken for business.
- **Entertainment.** Budgets for customer entertainment can easily be reduced or scaled back.

- **Meal subsidy.** Cafeteria service and catered lunches bought on the premises can be reduced or eliminated.

- **Travel.** Business-related travel can be replaced by teleconferences or video conferences, or at the minimum first-class airfare travel and expensive hotels should be shelved in favor of less costly options.

An important reason to consider cutting perquisites is morale. In general "perks" are provided to managers and senior leadership rather than the broad-based employee population. By reducing or cutting perquisites that are perceived as luxuries, the company is spreading the pain among all classes of employees. Senior leadership makes the point best when it states: "We all must share in tightening our belts during this crisis."

REDUCTION OR ELIMINATION OF 401(K) CONTRIBUTION

Most companies provide qualified profit-sharing programs and/or 401(k) programs as a benefit. In both cases the company makes a contribution. In the case of a 401(k) plan, the company may make a contribution as a "match" to the employee contributions.

Cutting the employer contribution is a reasonable place to cut costs. Reducing contributions can easily cut costs by 1 percent or more of payroll on an annual basis. However, there are some important issues senior leadership should consider before moving ahead with this option. First, cutting contributions requires modifying the legal documentation for a qualified benefit plan, which can take time and can be quite costly to execute. Second and more important, a 401(k) plan is a long-term benefit for a company, and changing it should be taken very seriously. It represents a long-term commitment to employees. Studies have shown that employees who take advantage of the employee matching contribution consider it an important part of their retirement planning. If the company expects the crisis to be short lived, then modifying the 401(k) plan could be more disruptive to the long-term employee than the company might want it to be.

REDUCTION OR SUSPENSION OF ANNUAL PAY INCREASES

Annual pay increases can be the same for all employees (e.g., an across-the-board amount or a cost-of-living adjustment). They can be distributed according to merit or performance or by means of some combination.

With the exception of situations where there is a binding union contract, senior leadership has substantial flexibility regarding the size and timing of annual pay increases. A typical annual increase budget is about 3 to 5 percent of base pay. Trimming the annual increase by 1 to 2 percent can put a big dent in the company's cost reduction requirement. In an extremely difficult cash crunch situation, the company could even consider completely suspending the annual increase. However, before slashing the annual pay increase budget, senior leadership should consider the following.

Maintaining Pay Competitiveness. Cutting back or suspending pay increases reduces the competitive level of pay. Furloughing the increase for 1 year may affect morale somewhat, but if there is a commitment to reinstate increases at a certain future date, the impact on morale will be minimized. Of course, withholding pay increases places the company in jeopardy, and headhunters will attempt to pick off attractive candidates for other expanding companies.

Losing the "Merit" in Merit Pay. Merit pay programs generally provide larger increases to higher level performers, and vice versa. If the annual increase budget is reduced to 2 percent of base pay or even lower, there is little room to reward above-average performers. It is almost impossible to reward excellent performers and, at the same time, spread the remainder of the budget to the great bulk of employees. If left with a small budget, it makes sense either to change the merit pay plan during the crisis to pay an across-the-board pay increase or to withhold increases, except to those few truly outstanding performers.

REDUCTION OR SUSPENSION OF BONUSES AND INCENTIVES

Bonuses and incentives may be self-correcting costs during a business crisis. If incentives are based on business performance targets at the corporate or operations level, then the poor performance that precipitated the crisis may result in attenuated incentive payments. Or simply put, no business, no bonus.

The places to look for cost cutting are in the areas of discretionary bonuses or other bonuses that are not dependent on reaching performance targets. These are the types of bonuses and incentives that are targets for reduction, suspension, or elimination.

At the same time, morale is an important consideration to take into account. Employees often consider bonuses a reward for longevity or loyalty. Some cash bonuses distributed regularly at the end of the fiscal year or during the holiday season are often considered by employees as a deferral of salary. Reducing or suspending these bonuses may be very disruptive to morale, so whether to cut these types of bonuses should be weighed against the severity of the crisis.

Finally, leaders should consider redirecting incentives instead of dropping them completely. As noted in Chapter 3, the turnaround bonus is an important way to motivate and keep key employees during a crisis. Without a way of positively directing efforts for future success, the company can create a self-defeating void.

HIRING FREEZE

The last cost-cutting strategy involves a freeze on hiring. A freeze reduces costs in two ways. Replacements for unfilled positions are not made, and replacements are not made for positions vacated after the freeze goes into effect. On this basis the company does not experience increased costs, and costs are reduced by attrition as people leave the company. Over time a hiring freeze may be a significant cost reduction. However, in actuality little is saved at the time of the immediate crisis. Nevertheless, this is a significant cost-cutting choice because it sends a clear message to employees about the seriousness of the situation and the need to focus on resolving the crisis.

HOW MUCH TIME WILL THE FIRST ROUND OF COST CUTTING TAKE?

Planning for Round 1 of cost cutting can be done quickly, in a matter of a few days. Implementation could take weeks, however, depending on how the company decides to proceed. Realizing the benefits can take longer because some savings come in a stream over a number of months. Furthermore, modifying the retirement program, the 401(k) plan, or initiating a voluntary severance plan can require substantial analysis, legal work, documentation, and mandated communication. Thus, what may be required is a time-phased plan that outlines the time frame for implementation of each cost reduction strategy along with an estimation of the stream of cost savings over time.

HOW MUCH COST CAN BE TAKEN OUT IN THE FIRST ROUND?

The 10 alternatives as well as other potential across-the-board cost-cutting measures will make a significant dent in the total cost reduction target. Some companies can stop at this point; others must seriously consider alternative work arrangements and layoffs. The biggest mistake an employer can make is to promise that there will be no layoffs when there may be a need to consider that option down the line. This is why it is critical to perform an analysis of all three rounds before committing to any particular strategy.

A NOTE ON EMPLOYEE INVOLVEMENT

Involvement of employees in developing cost-cutting opportunities will enhance the acceptance of solutions. This can mean brainstorming sessions, focus group meetings, regular staff meetings, suggestion hotlines, or other means the company may choose. Great caution should be taken involving employee input in the successive cost-cutting rounds because of the serious issues at stake, including job security.

SUMMARY

- Each of the 10 alternatives differs in the amount and time required to initiate and reduce cost.

- Senior leadership should be careful not to make promises it can't comply with since it may then lose credibility at a critical point.

- A number of cost-cutting alternatives, such as voluntary severance, are fraught with legal and regulatory potholes, so any should be undertaken with great caution and with the approval of the company's legal counsel.

CHAPTER 8

Step 5: Implement Alternative Work Arrangements

KEY PRINCIPLES

- Alternative work arrangements allow a company to retain critical human capital and at the same time reduce compensation costs.

- Costs incurred with alternative work arrangements are minimal and are far outweighed by the benefits.

- Novel supervision and management techniques are required to make alternative work arrangements run smoothly.

- Alternative work arrangements are not for every employee but for those with critical skills.

THE SECOND ROUND OF COST CUTTING: CREATIVE ALTERNATIVES TO LAYOFFS ARE WIN-WIN FOR THE COMPANY AND EMPLOYEES

Accenture (formerly Andersen Consulting) offered its employees an alternative work arrangement when it needed to cut costs. Workers had the chance to take a sabbatical at a nonprofit organization of their choice. Stephanie Braun jumped at the opportunity, even though it meant a temporary 80 percent reduction in pay. Braun, then 32, manager of Accenture's chemicals industry group, took a 7-month stint overseeing volunteers at the Fairy Godmother Foundation in Chicago, which grants wishes to the terminally ill 18 years and older. "It was an incredible chance to focus on something besides work, yet remain with the company. I had savings and am on my own so I could afford this," Braun said. She also used her time off to study to be a docent at the Chicago Architecture Foundation.

For Accenture the idea was an innovative but risky way to cut costs and retain employee talent for the long term. Dubbed "FlexLeave," the program began as a pilot for U.S. employees who had worked at Accenture for at least 12 months. Roughly 1200 of 17,000 eligible domestic employees initially signed on for the opportunity. Although they received only 20 percent of their salary, they continued to receive benefits and have use of their company laptops.

The Accenture story is typical of companies today that substitute traditional layoffs for custom-designed alternatives that maintain an employment relationship with the company at a reduced level for a period of time when business conditions do not warrant full-time employment. The results of such arrangements can be very rewarding and motivating to employees like Braun; it also helps the employer maintain its skill base and avoid separation transaction costs.

INNOVATIVE ALTERNATIVES ARE NOT BOUND BY INDUSTRY OR LOCATION

Companies in virtually every industry are adopting alternative work arrangements to cut costs and keep their best people. Following are some examples of companies that have adopted innovative solutions.

QualxServ, a 1000-employee firm headquartered in Tewksbury, Massachusetts, with 30 district offices throughout the United States, has implemented cost controls with layoffs as a last resort. The privately held company services PCs and laptops for contracted clients. Linda Lamonakis, human resources manager, U. S. operations, pointed out that the company has restructured the organization with the appropriate regular and contingent work force to run the business effectively.

Employees were amenable to reductions in costs in lieu of losing their jobs. The contract staff was furloughed during the Thanksgiving/Christmas holidays when call volume was lower. There was a vacation buyback program twice during the last 2 years, and the firm was considering reducing carryover vacation time. In addition, the company changed the way it paid for standby time and reduced overtime expenses by implementing various workshifts.

A regional medical center in Central Florida created a "transition staffing pool" for those whose jobs were eliminated. The nonprofit single-site acute care regional medical center employs 3400. They have seasonal fluctuations in staff needs and have also restructured a number of departments. As a result some employees were displaced and required reassignment.

The transition staffing pool works in the following way: First vacancies are posted, and then employees in the pool have the option to bid for transfer to other departments. If they don't want to accept a different assignment, they are paid for 3 months severance. At the end of that time, they are terminated.

The medical center tries to avoid layoffs because of a limited talent pool in the area. They don't want to terminate talented people when it's difficult to find them in the first place. This program has been very successful.

Life Cell Corporation in Branchburg, New Jersey, is a biotech firm with 150 employees. Facing a layoff, the firm went with across-the-board cost cutting. It solicited volunteers for layoffs with severance packages, cross-trained employees to fill open positions internally, monitored overtime to divide workload more evenly, which provided work for those who might otherwise have been laid off, and budgeted for attrition (not replacing those who left).

It then combined layoffs with alternative work arrangements. Management sent a directive to the employees that said: "We have extra work in this department. If you try a new job, it will keep you occupied and perhaps save a layoff." It behooved the employees to learn different skills. It was also a good chance for their career development to learn more than one job. They were told that cross training would benefit them, at Life Cell and in their future career.

THE FOUR ALTERNATIVE WORK ARRANGEMENTS

There are four generic types of alternative work arrangements most companies use today. In actual use these programs have a wide variety of applications and combine some features of the generic programs. Overall, a review of the following four approaches will provide guidance regarding features that might be applied in a company. These four approaches, in conjunction with layoffs and other compensation cost-cutting measures, provide a number of ways to retain employees as productive and active members of a business, albeit at a reduced level of involvement and compensation. Following is an overview of the alternative work arrangements and their potential benefits and costs. (Discussion of alternatives as a cost-cutting choice was presented in Chapter 5.)

JOB/SKILL SHARING

Job sharing and/or skill sharing involves reducing staff members to part-time status with the sharing of responsibilities and duties for a single job function. With such an arrangement it's necessary for the job sharers to collaborate with each other to communicate progress on work that is shared, and also keep the job sharers informed of transactions and events that occur during each other's "off time." Job sharing can mean split days, split weeks, or any other combination that makes sense. Work can be accomplished on a common site or through telework arrangements (i.e., communications with the job sharer and the company site through networked computers, teleconferencing, and video conferencing). Table 8-1 summarizes the costs and benefits of job sharing.

Table 8-1   Job/Skill Sharing

Benefits to the company	Retention of human capital investments
	Continuity in key job functions by experienced staff
	Maintenance of important skill sets on the job
Benefits to the employee	Income continuation at a reduced salary and maintenance of relationship with employer
	Ability to post for a full-time assignment
	Opportunity to learn new skill sets
Costs to the company	Continuation of compensation at reduced level
Costs to the employee	Reduction in salary
Salary and benefits	Base pay reduced in proportion to reduction from full-time work
	Maintenance of benefits (at a reduced level if there is a different program for part-time status)
Where it works best	Any position or department

Benefits to the Company. The greatest benefit of job/skill sharing is the retention of human capital. Every two job sharers include one employee who could have been laid off. These arrangements also allow for continuity of employment for staff even though the job assignments of the job sharers might be different from previous job responsibilities. In fact employees are placed in positions to broaden their skill base.

Benefits to the Employee. In the short term, the employee benefits from income continuation. Even at a reduction of up to 50 percent, the continuation of benefits is a major advantage to the employee and cushions the blow of reduced base pay income. In the long run, maintaining a relationship with the company has numerous benefits, including priority status on postings for full-time positions when they become available. There is also the benefit of remaining part of the company and keeping abreast of current events. Finally, there is the opportunity to learn new skill sets and broaden personal capabilities.

Costs to the Company. The company incurs the cost of compensation, benefits, and overhead for all employees currently at work. However, the base compensation is significantly reduced for the job sharers. The major short-term financial benefits accrue from the lack of severance costs. By eliminating one job (that is now shared by two people) the company reduces the total cost of one salary but not the benefits package. At the same time, the company does not incur separation costs, which can amount to the cost of benefits for one person for 1 year. These two cost items in effect cancel each other out during the first year.

Costs to the Employee. The obvious straightforward cost to the employee is a reduction in salary. There is also a change in status. There are potential feelings of shame for having lost a full-time position (even temporarily) as well as anger with the employer or the world in general. In addition, feelings of insecurity are driven by loss of income and unfamiliarity with a changed position that is thrust onto the employee. Of course, the alternative is the complete loss of one's job, but people don't necessarily act rationally in these situations. Consequently, this work arrangement is not for everyone.

Salary and Benefits. Salary is reduced by 50 percent for job sharers who are evenly splitting responsibilities. Beyond salary, numerous types of arrangements can be established that make sense for particular job functions. Work can be done on a common site or on two or more sites. Sometimes job sharers telecommute.

Dealing with benefits may be a challenge. Many companies require a minimum number of hours worked in a year for an employee to qualify for health and welfare benefits. If the job sharing arrangement takes time worked below the minimum and benefits are not available, then a major source of motivation for an employee to accept job sharing may be negated. Therefore, to establish job sharing (or other alternative work arrangements), it will be necessary to research and determine the accessibility of health and welfare benefits and provide them if at all possible.

Where It Works Best. Job sharing can work anywhere in an organization, and it can work at any level from the executive suite to entry-level positions. What is important is that the work can be split between two or more individuals in a reasonable way and that there is frequent and clear communication between job sharers.

CONTRACTING ARRANGEMENTS

Companies use contracting arrangements when there is a service that can be provided to an organization by an independent person, agency, or organization more economically than employing the resources directly. In addition, truly independent contractors must supply the services to avoid conflict with the legal status of a contractor versus an employee. For example, merely moving an individual from the company's payroll to contract status does not necessarily establish a contracting relationship. The company would still have the responsibility of an employer, including offering all required benefit programs, payroll taxes, and so forth. However, contracting arrangements are reasonable for services in areas such as accounting, human resources, engineering, marketing, or any other function where specialized expertise can be externally supplied. The contractor must act as an independent business and keep financial records, reporting, and filing with state and federal agencies, including income taxes and sales taxes as applicable.

The appeal of contracting as an alternative work arrangement is that the employer can offer the former employee a chance to provide services and expertise on a part-time or hourly basis and the company maintains the use of the skills and capabilities of that employee. The former employee as an independent contractor can also offer services to other employers and agencies at the same time. Following is an overview of benefits and costs of this alternative work arrangement, which is summarized in Table 8-2.

Table 8-2   Contracting Arrangements

Benefits to the company	Continuity of important services
	Maintenance of company-specific knowledge
Benefits to the employee	Income continuation
	Maintenance of skills
Costs to the company	Continuation of compensation
Costs to the employee	Loss of regular employment status with the company
	Cost of running the contract business
Salary and benefits	Termination of salary and change to contract arrangements
	Change in employment status that generally results in termination of employee benefits
Where it works best	Specialized services that can be supplied independent from an employment relationship

Benefits to the Company. The major benefits to the company are a continuity of services from individuals who have critical company knowledge. With a contracting arrangement, the company can reduce headcount yet have available the accumulated skills and competencies of specialists. However, the former employees must be motivated to continue providing services, and payment for their services must be competitive.

Benefits to the Employee. There are many benefits to the employee. Besides income continuation, the contracting arrangement is an opportunity to broaden skills. In effect the contractor can build a new career as a contract consultant to other companies in addition to the former employer.

Costs to the Company. The main cost to the company is continuation of compensation, although at a reduced level from the former total employee compensation costs. The actual pay arrangements can be quite different. For example, consider a marketing specialist with an annual salary of $60,000 and $15,000 in benefits for a total compensation of $75,000. If she becomes a contractor for approximately one-quarter of the time, or 10 hours per week, the cost to the employer would likely exceed $18,750, or 25 percent of former compensation. The total cost might range from $25,000 to $30,000 to cover overhead, the provision of government mandated benefits, and self-supplied health and welfare benefits.

Costs to the Employee. The former employee would receive lower total compensation from the employer if he or she worked as a contractor on a part-time basis. In addition, the former employee as a new contractor would provide all costs associated with doing business, including overhead expenses such as an office computer and telephone. (But these are tax deductions for the independent contractor.) The biggest expense would be for starting up the contract business.

Salary and Benefits. The change in status to contractor in almost all cases will result in termination of health and welfare benefits. The contractor supplies these benefits. This may be an insurmountable hurdle for some individuals who do not wish to set up their own business, supply benefits, and make their own reports to the federal and state governments.

Where It Works Best. Specialized services that require unique expertise are typically provided on a contract basis.

FURLOUGHED OFFSITE NET WORKERS

This work force arrangement is a new approach made possible by recent innovations in telecommunications technology. Work time and salary are reduced by up to 70 percent or more for employees whose skills are critical in the long term, but where short-term full-time employment is not economical. (See Table 8-3.) This staff is provided telecom equipment for their homes. They are told to check in and communicate via telework on a regular basis and are on call for short-term assignments or consultations. The employee is free to

Table 8-3   Furloughed Offsite Net Workers

Benefits to the company	Retention of human capital and critical skills and competencies.
Benefits to the employee	Income continuation (at reduced salary)
	Maintenance of relationship with the company
	Ability to post for a new assignment
Costs to the company	Salary cost for an "on-call" employee
Costs to the employee	Cost to set up and maintain teleworking equipment
	Not working in a regular job on a day-to-day basis
	Reduced income
Salary and benefits	Continuation of base pay at a reduced rate
	Maintenance of benefits (at a reduced level if there is a different program for part-time employees)
Where it works best	Knowledge workers

work elsewhere within the boundaries of a noncompetition agreement. This arrangement can be for an open- or closed-ended time period.

Benefits to the Company. The main benefit to the company is the retention of critical skills during a slack work period. If the down period is expected to be less than 18 months, it is much more economical to retain skills in this fashion than to lay off the employee, experience short-term separation costs, and then turn around and expend more than a year's salary to hire and train a new employee.

Benefits to the Employee. The furloughed employee remains a part of the organization at a greatly reduced level of activity. Through use of remote "teleworking" stations, the employee remains in touch via the company's telecommunications networks. Usually this requires approximately a 20 to 30 percent time commitment. In this manner the employee keeps up to date on the progress of various projects and events. He or she also is on call to participate in projects requiring specific expertise or skill. When openings for positions become available, the furloughed employee is notified and has the opportunity to post for the opening. In addition, health and welfare benefits remain available as they were before the furlough began. These arrangements are generally for a specific period of time before they end or restart.

Costs to the Company. There are two types of costs to the company. First, there is the straightforward cost of salary at a reduced level and benefits. Second, telecom costs are required to maintain network communications. These latter costs can run from providing laptops for affected employees to setting up complete work stations in homes.

Costs to the Employee. The costs to the employee include reduced income for the period of time on furlough. In addition, the employer may require a formal written agreement that restricts certain types of employment (i.e., with a competitor) and confidentiality of proprietary company information for the length of the furlough. Furthermore, due to the change in employment status, the employee may be angry or embarrassed.

Salary and Benefits. Salary is continued at a significantly lower rate, but health and welfare benefits are maintained.

Where It Works Best. Furlough arrangements should be used for knowledge workers who have critical information or experience with proprietary methodologies. These are generally found in the information technology area but may also be part of marketing, manufacturing or engineering, or other functions in the company.

TEMPORARY ASSIGNMENTS

This work force arrangement enables staffing of strategic projects by employees with specialized skills on an "assignment" basis. (See Table 8-4.) With this alternative employees lose their regular job but not their employment. This relationship can be either full or part

Table 8-4 Temporary Assignments

Benefits to the company	Retention of critical human capital at a reduced cost when employment is less than full time
	Critical projects don't fall by the wayside
Benefits to the employee	Income continuation at reduced salary
	Maintenance of relationship with the company
	Opportunity to post for new assignments
Costs to the company	Salary and benefits
Costs to the employee	Previous job is replaced with assignment status and reduced income
	Long-term employment in jeopardy
Salary and benefits	If the time commitment of the employee is reduced, the salary is reduced proportionally
	Benefits status remains the same unless time commitment changes employee to part-time status, triggering a benefits change
Where it works best	Where specific value-added projects can be identified

time, and employment becomes a series of project assignments. In effect, the employee's role becomes one of in-house consultant.

Benefits to the Company. This approach retains human capital for the company similar to furloughed net workers, but employees are placed on actual projects that involve greater time and salary commitment. Usually the employee works about 50 percent of the time and is assigned to a specific project requiring on-site involvement.

Benefits to the Employee. As with other arrangements the main benefits to the employee involve continuing employment, health and welfare benefits, and the opportunity to post for full-time assignments.

Cost to the Company. The main costs to a company are salary and benefits. The employee on assignment typically has a reduction in salary for an indefinite period.

Costs to the Employee. The full-time job is replaced by part-time assignments with reduced compensation and benefits. In addition, continuing employment is contingent on the actual temporary assignment. When work is completed, new assignments replace the completed ones, or the employee no longer remains in employment.

Salary and Benefits. Salary is reduced to a level commensurate with the time requirements for the assignment, usually 50 percent or less of a regular salary. Health and welfare benefits are provided.

Where It Works Best. Wherever there is a need for a special assignment with critical skills, temporary assignments are a viable alternative.

EMPLOYEE SKILLS AND COMPETENCIES NEEDED

A number of personal characteristics facilitate an effective transition to contract status, to an offsite Net worker, to a special assignment, or to a job share situation. These personal characteristics all relate to the ability to work independently from a supervisor and share work with peers:

- **Self-starting.** Ability to work under minimal supervision for long stretches of time.

- **Time management and self-scheduling.** Ability to organize own work and schedule activities.

- **Teamwork.** Ability to work effectively on multiple in-person and virtual teams.

- **Information technology.** Ability to troubleshoot and maintain own equipment.

MANAGEMENT AND SUPERVISORY SKILLS NEEDED

Alternative work arrangements also represent a big change for many managers and supervisors. Under the circumstances, they must manage two people sharing a job, work with contractors rather than regular employees, and delegate employees from a distant, remote location. This calls for openness, flexibility, and the ability to learn new supervisory skills. Managers who are used to frequent in-person progress checks and "looking over their employees' shoulders" may have difficulty adapting to these new situations. A number of new skills are needed to match the required management and supervisory skills, including:

- **Adapting styles to telecommunications from face-to-face interactions.** Getting comfortable with less frequent face-to-face meetings and learning ways to effectively communicate remotely.

- **Providing latitude for technical specialists to use their expertise to solve problems independently.** Learning how to delegate problem solving, again in remote locations.

- **Less frequent check-in on work progress.** Adapting a style to review progress on a project with longer time intervals, sometimes called *timespan of discretion.* This is a skill for managing a project with fewer interim reviews.

The most important difference is that the pace of work changes from daily cycles of supervisory and management review to cycles of longer duration, sometimes up to a month for review.

WHAT TO EXPECT WITH ALTERNATIVE WORK ARRANGEMENTS

Although not a panacea, alternative work arrangements should soften the blow of reductions and keep the key people and skills needed to thrive in the future. Remember, it's important not only to cut costs now, but also to invest in the future. Following is a list of improvements that should be expected:

- **Sharp reduction in short-term separation costs.** Every job saved will reduce separation costs by an average of about 20 to 25 percent of annual salary.

- **Retention of key people.** If people with targeted skills and capabilities are chosen, the firm has a better chance to retain the best people and critical skills in an environment of forced reductions and layoffs.

- **Higher morale replacing fear and anxiety.** The company has a much better chance of rallying the troops in an environment where it outwardly demonstrates the desire to maintain a core cadre of people to succeed in the short and long term.

- **Reduction in future hiring and staffing costs.** By keeping key people and skills now, future ramp-up costs drop significantly.

SUMMARY

- Alternative work arrangements are a powerful cost-cutting and human capital preservation tool.

- Each type of work arrangement (job/skill sharing, contracting, furloughs, and special assignments) helps retain good people. An organization should explore all options to decide which ones work best.

- Even though the benefits greatly outweigh the costs in theory, making alternative work arrangements successful requires changes in the way a company selects and manages its people, including how its supervisors manage employees in their departments.

- Before proceeding too far in considering alternative work arrangements, an organization should conduct a pro forma analysis to project the balance of benefits versus costs.

CHAPTER 9

Step 6: Implement Layoffs

KEY PRINCIPLES

- Handled poorly, layoffs damage the morale of survivors. In addition, they can provoke violence and negative public exposure, which makes rehiring harder in the future.

- Those remaining must be encouraged and rewarded to stay through the bad times with a combination of strategies, including financial compensation and other forms of rewards and recognition.

- It is wise to implement a public relations campaign to explain the company's need for layoffs.

THE THIRD ROUND OF COST CUTTING

It was about 9 A.M. when Danny L., a 34-year-old middle manager with an international food service company headquartered on the East Coast, pulled his red Jeep into the parking lot behind his office. He sat glumly behind the wheel thinking about the meeting he faced that morning with his supervisor with whom he had worked for 4 years. The ax had come down on several people in his division. Rumors were flying that more layoffs were imminent. Sales in the firm were shaky, revenue was shrinking, losses were posted, and efforts to develop new convenience frozen-food products had failed. Would Danny become the next layoff in his division? He had recently married, and he and his wife had made a down payment on a pricey condominium. Danny's intuition was correct.

The firing was handled with so much emotion that both he and his boss ended up sitting in shock after the news was delivered. "Danny, I know this is a tough time for you, and I hate to do this. It stinks, but I've been given no choice. Who knows? I could be next if things don't get better, or maybe I won't stay. I'm sending out my résumé as well."

Both men stared at one another. Danny's eyes began to swell with tears; he blinked hard, and turned away. His boss reached out to offer some support; Danny turned farther away. "I guess I'll go collect the stuff in my desk," he said, looking down.

His boss put a hand on his colleague's shoulder, "Give me a call and we can meet. I know I can help you. I probably can convince the right people to offer you some outplacement help. Give me some more time, and I probably can get the right folks in the company eventually to hire you back. I also know people at the company who know people, who probably could help get you a job or at least some introductions at the right companies. Of course, you will get good written recommendations. Let's get together for a drink when you're up for it."

Danny rose, headed for the door, and continued looking away. He was upset and embarrassed. Although the boss was taking the right step emotionally and trying to offer support, his verbal efforts went overboard and were unprofessional. First, he made too many promises out of concern for his staff member but without the authorization of senior leadership. He told Danny that he probably could get outplacement help, that he probably could get rehired when the economy came back, and that he would have job options elsewhere, in part due to recommendations from company personnel.

Even more significant, Danny's boss didn't tell the truth. He hid the real reason for the termination. The company was in a cash crunch and had to cut back. Danny's skills were expendable because his department was not terribly busy at that point. His boss was honest in explaining the poor company results that necessitated the layoffs, but he didn't share the news that the company felt it should get rid of those like Danny without mission-critical skills.

In letting Danny go, his boss, who had never fired anyone before, said the wrong things—said too much—and behaved unprofessionally. In such cases it would have been better if he had carefully recited the termination communication from a piece of paper word for word, sentence for sentence to maintain consistency, meet legal guidelines, and ensure that the message was delivered correctly. The termination could have gone like this:

> As a result of the reorganization and the company's efforts to control costs, your employment with our company is being terminated and your job is also being eliminated. The decision is effective immediately, and it is a final decision. There is some important information I need to give you that has to do with pay and benefits. Outplacement services have been retained for you at the ABC firm. Here is a folder detailing your benefits and services. You are to leave the building after

you collect your personal belongings. If you need to return for any reason, please call to arrange for an appointment. Do you have any questions for me at this time? If I don't have the answers now, I can get back to you with answers shortly.

This scripted message should clearly specify the intentions of the company and events that will take place relative to termination. In some cases the employee is asked to leave on the spot like Danny; in others the employee is asked to stay on for weeks or even months. In any event the message should avoid unwarranted promises or personal opinions that do not reflect the policies of the company.

THE HARDEST THING A MANAGER WILL EVER DO

Ask a manager or company head about the hardest tasks they'll tackle in their jobs, and invariably they'll list as one of them laying off or eliminating employees. It may mean many sleepless nights for them or, worse, constant second-guessing on what they could have done differently and what they still might have to do in the future.

One manager relates her saga. Fran Keeth, president, Shell Chemical L.P., headquartered in Houston, according to a January 20, 2002, article in the *New York Times*, reported that she threw up in the bathroom after announcing plant closings and firings. She felt it was the worst week of her life. She was working in Shell's products business, oil and chemicals, as the finance general manager. She had only worked at the job 3 to 4 months, and because of financial problems the company had to reorganize. She and two colleagues were asked to come up with a plan. The plan called for them to reduce staff by 25 percent. Shell had nine operating facilities in the United States, and Keeth and her colleagues spent 1 week going to every location to tell workers personally what was going on.

At each location they told workers that the company was closing the facility or selling it and that nobody would continue to work for Shell. Employees' reactions ranged from acceptance to shock and anger. She believed the great diversity of reactions was due to the fact that Shell was not good at that time when it came to communicating its financial outlook. Many employees thought the company had a lot of money. People called her names.

At another company, an East Coast compensation director tells how his firm tried to avert layoffs. But the inevitable happened. He found it to be pure hell. "We told employees via e-mail that economic pressures would be overwhelming. We didn't know how rough. We cried in July it was so hard. We couldn't get our numbers up, our routines together. It was like recovering from a stroke—very painful, slow, and it hurt. At first the system does a lot of the work. The nonperformers take themselves out. Pressure takes them out. But anytime somebody leaves, you feel the loss. Even the deadwood. It's the ones with talent who are really tough to lose. But even losing dead-wood is tough because you spend a lot of time and money training, teaching, and motivating new hires."

Laying off employees is never a pleasant task, but it does not have to be acrimonious if companies are upfront and honest about the reasons they are necessary and if they follow all effective procedural rules and legal regulations. The person handling the layoff should try to experience the feelings of the employees receiving the bad news. How this is handled will impact the reputation of the company as an employer. The company should lay off staff in such a way that the employees severed are not embarrassed in front of colleagues when they have to pack up and walk out of their offices and the company with their belongings.

A Massachusetts-based technology company has this prescription for conducting layoffs:

A layoff is done in one day. When it is determined, section managers notify the employee the day of the action. The employee is called aside to an office to minimize the impact on the employee. He's walked down to an area where HR reviews a severance package with him. This includes outplacement (a person is on site) and someone from the temporary agency who helps the employee find new employment. The employee is then asked to leave that day. The approach is scripted. Some people have never done a layoff before, and they're uncomfortable about what to say.

Being laid off is somewhat akin to experiencing a serious illness or death. The employee goes through a cycle of grief from depression to anger and needs to work through these emotions at his or her own pace. Moreover, mishandling a layoff can result in huge costs to the company, both tangible and intangible. These may include expensive lawsuits, sabotage and even violence in the workplace among disgruntled employees. An example is a man in Los Angeles who worked at a nuclear power plant. He was laid off and threatened to retaliate. The FBI investigated and found an arsenal of weapons in his possession. Or there's the story about the commissary in Houston where laid-off employees tainted the food.

To deal with terminated employees in a humane, straightforward, and effective way, consider the following guidelines.

RULE 1: COMMUNICATE IN A DIGNIFIED AND RESPECTFUL WAY

Laying off an employee, whether scripted or not, should be done with tact and dignity to show that the company values its employees in bad times as well as in good times. There was a good reason that the person was hired, so it makes sense to treat people with the same dignity and respect on their way out.

When conducting layoffs, managers should try not to burn bridges. When it's time to ramp up, the firm may want to rehire some employees who were laid off. This means, in addition to offering a reasonable severance package, not bad-mouthing anyone let go, not doing anything construed as illegal, and always leaving the door open for the future. Several company examples point this up vividly.

One company bungled layoffs. The firm forced employees to resign by taking away phones and demoting them from managers to food service workers. Some were so humiliated that they became physically ill. One man reported that he sat at his desk every day with no workers. The stress was so severe that he had a nervous breakdown. This firm set itself up for expensive lawsuits.

In another example an ERISA specialist and attorney with a major midwestern corporation was told in October that massive layoffs were necessary. But the layoffs weren't planned until December and weren't put into effect until March. The time frame took months. The firm finally let the attorney go on a Friday at the end of March, but had not found a replacement law firm to do his work. So they called him the next Monday morning and rehired him for 3 months on a contract basis.

Although he was reluctant to go back at first—his pride had been wounded—he quickly realized the company would pay him more per month for those 3 months than they had paid him the month before. He took the money—and the job.

This is not unusual. People are let go without adequate planning and are brought back as consultants or on a contract basis, often at a higher salary. Some companies have to rehire employees they recently laid off.

RULE 2: CAREFULLY CHOOSE THE PLACE AND TIME TO CONDUCT THE LAYOFF

Choosing the place and time for the termination discussion is a critical factor in the lasting impression made on those who will leave, and it contributes to the quality and dignity of the experience.

The best approach for the place to communicate such news may vary depending on the person, the physical location of the office, and the economic circumstances. Some companies prefer to tackle layoffs in one-on-one sessions, and others prefer to communicate with a group of employees. There are also combinations of approaches. For example, in one case a human resources manager had to eliminate 14 people in one department. He called them together. The head of the division, department head, supervisor, HR director, and top management together presented the rationale and the way the layoffs would be implemented over the next few weeks. Employees then met one on one to deal with specifics. In another case all meetings were held on a one-on-one basis in complete confidentiality. Table 9-1 summarizes the pros and cons of the different approaches

The personal meeting is the most effective way to communicate the bad news of a layoff, if the communicator has the skill and presence of mind to keep the discussion on track and professional. Many companies have human resources or legal staff present to avoid future claims

Table 9-1 Alternative Ways to Communicate a Layoff

Approach	Pro	Con
Large Group Meeting	Ability to personally communicate with a large number of people at one time with a consistent message	Lacks one-on-one contact
Small Group Meeting	Ability to have a more intimate group discussion	Lacks one-on-one contact
Individual Meeting	Effective way to communicate clearly and directly	Potential for confrontation or misspeaking

regarding things that were allegedly said in the meeting but disputed later. (This is the reason for a script in some companies.) The presence of such professionals also can ensure that all of the pertinent information is covered in a fair, consistent, and equitable way.

The more impersonal the setting, the greater the distaste and sense of disrespect felt by affected employees. A combination of the alternatives often works best for an employer. But with additional meetings the issue of timing and advance notice arises. Timing can range from immediate notification with the requirement to leave the premises to providing days to weeks of advance notice. Table 9-2 outlines alternatives for advance notice.

There is no hard-and-fast rule for advance notice timing. A lot depends on the culture of the company, its current situation, and its prior experience. One example is a medical reprocessing company, which gave employees who were laid off 1 to 2 weeks' severance and the chance to come back when needed. Each supervisor met with those who directly reported to him or her to communicate the changes. The CEO met with small groups to discuss the company status a week later. The HR director discussed how a reduction in staff was required

Table 9-2   Advance Notice for Layoff

Approach	Pro	Con
Immediate Notice Prior to Escort off the Premises	Avoids negative behavior and sabotage "Surgical separation" of employees	Anger and shame Employees are less likely to return in the future No sense of closure for an employee
Short -Term Notice— 2 Weeks	Advance notice for graceful exit Employee has the ability to do some advance planning	Potential negative work environment and productivity fall off Uncomfortable environment for everyone Potential disruptive behavior
Long-Term Notice	Employee has the ability to do advance planning	Magnifying the "cons" of short-term notice

because growth plans had not met expectations. She gave each employee a letter explaining the layoff, said the company would not contest unemployment filings, and included severance explanations and COBRA arrangements.

In another case the layoff discussion became the final discussion, as in the case of Danny. The manager escorted the employee to his office to collect his personal items and then from the building with instructions not to return. This harsh treatment is sometimes required when there is concern about sabotage, revenge, or theft of confidential information. It certainly does not enhance a feeling of warmth and caring toward the company.

At the end of the day, a company must choose a method that fits with its culture and its approach to employee relationships. A company that has a close and personal relationship with employees should carefully consider the long-term implications of changing its "face" to employees in a layoff situation.

RULE 3: BE CAREFUL WHAT YOU SAY IN A ONE-ON-ONE DISCUSSION

The main reason companies script the layoff discussion or have professional staff present is to ensure that nothing is said that would haunt the company later. Managers should not make promises they can't keep, such as hinting at hopes to rehire the employee if it is not the company's policy. They should not answer questions off-the-cuff if they are unsure of the answers. Finally, managers should, at all costs, avoid confrontations with employees.

There is always the desire to cushion the blow of a layoff, somehow staving off the finality of the event. However, once the company has made its decisions, it is not appropriate in any way to misdirect the employee regarding the harsh reality of the situation. It is best for everyone to accept the situation and move forward.

RULE 4: ABIDE BY LEGAL AND REGULATORY GUIDELINES

There are definite ways to avoid legal and regulatory pitfalls. Before conducting layoffs compile a list of who is to be laid off, secure personal evaluations and other relevant data regarding those on the list, determine final severance packages far in advance, know federal and state regulations and abide by them, and be sure that the criteria used to prepare for the layoffs are uniform throughout the company.

The goal is to have a plan that benefits rather than hurts a company. In turn the company should be fair, open, and honest toward employees to keep its reputation intact and to avoid spending dollars on costly legal battles. A company may need to undertake more work upfront, but the intangible cost savings and the goodwill generated will be enormously worthwhile. There are several potential minefields to bear in mind.

Worker Adjustment and Retraining Act (WARN).[1] If a plant closing is imminent that involves layoffs, a federal plant closing law called the Worker Adjustment and Retraining Act (WARN) protects employees from unlawful plant closings and mass layoffs without notice. It requires employers to give at least 60 days notice to affected employees, their representative, and state and local officials. Those covered include employers who have at least 100 full-time workers on staff. A plant closing means a shutdown resulting in unemployment during any 30-day period for 50 or more employees.

Other provisions define an employment loss as an involuntary separation: a layoff exceeding 6 months or a reduction in work hours of more than 50 percent during each month of any 6-month period. WARN also covers what constitutes a mass layoff. This is a reduction in the work force that is not linked to a plant closing and results in an employment loss during any 30-day period for at least 33 percent of

---

[1.] Paul Cherner, Partner in Altheimer & Gray's Labor Law Practice in Chicago, Illinois, contributed to this section.

the full-time employees or at least 50 full-time employees at a single site in a 30-day period.

If handled incorrectly under WARN, a company can end up owing several hundred thousand dollars in back pay and benefits under the employee benefit plan for the period during the violation. Some states have their own version of WARN. Be sure that legal counsel is aware of the WARN rules that apply.

A company that partially closed a plant in Virginia moved the operations portion of the business to another site in Massachusetts. Employees were impacted by the move, but the company had to give 60-days notice because of the WARN act that affected more than 50 employees. The move was complicated and took place in a number of steps over a year-long period. Some employees immediately moved with the plant, others were laid off, and a third group faced a delayed move almost a year later. There were a number of layoff packages and retention agreements, with the requirement for continuous communication by the company to comply with WARN. (See the last section of this chapter for sample compliance letters.)

Employee Discrimination. The Equal Employment Opportunity Commission (EEOC) protects employees against unlawful discrimination in cases of layoffs and terminations. Claims of discrimination are generally based on a worker showing that he or she was a member of a protected class, had performed at the level of the employer's legitimate expectations, was discharged or demoted, and others not in the protected class were treated more favorably. The employer must demonstrate a legitimate nondiscriminatory basis for a layoff decision, and it must have clearly established and consistently applied criteria.

Regardless of how many are laid off, the employer needs to use uniform criteria and be able to defend them in making layoff selections. Layoffs that affect one group more than others disproportionately should be seriously scrutinized. It makes sense to take snapshots of the work force and groups that the firm plans to lay off. Then it makes sense to take snapshots again of the groups and people left behind. Does something jump out that's unusual? If so, the company should go back through the layoff lists to ensure that criteria for the decisions were made fairly and can be defended. If the company conducts a human capital analysis, such as the approach described in Chapter 5, it will have such criteria available. The important point to remember is that your actions should be consistent and based on fairly applied job-based criteria.

Older Workers Benefit Protection Act (OWBPA). This law applies to situations where employers offer severance packages to older workers (age 40 and above), including those who may qualify for early retirement. The OWBPA requires companies to communicate with employees regarding their rights in an open and noncoercive way. When employees are offered these special severance arrangements, it is advisable that they be asked to sign a waiver regarding not filing a future claim on employment discrimination. The OWBPA specifies how this should be done. (See Appendix A and B for Sample Agreements.)

Unions. Federal laws protect unions and their collective bargaining agreements. The employer cannot abrogate a valid contract, and must follow the procedures specified in the contract for layoffs. The employer must bargain with the union over wages, hours, and other terms and conditions of employment. Most collective bargaining agreements require layoffs in reverse seniority, resulting in the inability on the company's part to retain workers who may have the required skills but less seniority. An employer cannot close one of its plants or lay off employees for the purpose of avoiding dealing with a union.

RULE 5: IMMEDIATELY TURN YOUR ATTENTION TO THE SURVIVORS

The patience of top performing employees who remain after the layoffs could wear thin if an employer announces another layoff, and maybe even another. For the employer, retaining talented survivors is likely to be tougher with each successive work force cut. After a second or third round of layoffs, employees get the picture very clearly, feel more insecure, and may start job hunting by sending out their résumés and networking with friends or former employers.

Listening to survivors and managers talk provides insight into the trauma they experience, which many do not realize until they're the ones left behind. Most echo similar thoughts or slight variations on the same advice.

The compensation manager at a Maryland company found the hardest step was deciding what to do with those who survived and deciding whether the company cut deeply enough into its ranks. He had to focus on enthusiasm when telling employees that there is good work here and your contribution is valued. He also told them that work would return.

In Judy Colyn's experience as human resources manager at Life Cell Corp., leaders maintain the dignity of the employees who are laid off to give the survivors security. They explain why a cut is made and that everything is taken into consideration so it isn't necessary to cut again in a month or two.

To build credibility after a small or mass layoff or a second or third round of cuts, company leaders should take three steps:

1. Continue frequent communications regarding progress the company is making.
2. Support the communications with rewards and recognition for top performers.
3. Begin rebuilding on the valued knowledge and skill remaining in the company.

THE EMPLOYEE VIEW OF LAYOFFS[2]

A national survey of 1214 laid off white-collar workers was conducted to gain an understanding of company practices regarding employees

2. Survey conducted by Jennifer L. Todd, and Chris Ryan, Senior Manager of Anderson's Human Capital Practice in conjunction with Vault, Inc.

who had been recently laid off (more than 70 percent of the respondents were laid off within 4 months of the survey). Employees averaged approximately $75,000 total annual income before the layoff, with an average age of approximately 30 years. The typical industries represented were finance, consulting, and legal fields. Table 9-3 provides insight into employee attitudes regarding the conduct of layoffs.

Understanding employee attitudes is critical to gain a clear picture of the lasting impression and reputation of the company. The more consistent the business practices of the company, the more the following will occur: more personal communications methods, better reasons communicated, fewer security measures required, and better employee attitudes regarding the employer. At the same time extreme measures requiring people to leave immediately are sometimes necessary to meet company security objectives. In summary, the company must consider the impact on employee attitudes when establishing the layoff process.

THE SEVERANCE PACKAGE

Simply stated, a severance package is a payment given to an employee "severed" from the company, whether due to a downsizing, layoff, or termination without cause. Voluntary severance agreements are covered

Table 9-3   Reactions of Employees to Layoffs

Layoff Process Element	Practices Associated with Positive Attitudes toward the Company	Practices Associated with Negative Attitudes toward the Company
Communication Method	One-on-one discussion	Phone call or voice mail
Communication of Reason for the Layoff	Company effectively communicated reasons	Company did not effectively communicate reasons
Security Measures Taken	None	Doors locked
Time Allowed to Remain	4 weeks +	Asked to leave immediately
Layoff Consistent with Typical Practice of Company	Consistent	Inconsistent

in Chapter 7. In that chapter severance payments are discussed as an incentive to leave the company. The severance package here relates to involuntary layoffs or terminations.

Severance payments can include a few weeks of extended paid salary, allowing the employee to search for a new job, or a lump sum the company pays to apologize for the disappointment and inconvenience for being laid off. Severance packages can include unpaid bonuses, stock options, an extension of medical benefits, and a contract with an outplacement firm. (An outplacement firm is a professional organization that helps employees rewrite their résumés, and practice interviewing, offers a phone number and fax number for potential employers to send important information, and provides a place for the employee to search the Internet for a position.)

Often companies will base the nature and size of the components of a severance package on the employee's pay level, tenure, or hierarchical level in the company. Typically, it is standard to offer nonexempt employees a few weeks of pay, allowing the employee to search for a new position while having some income during the search. Senior managers typically can expect 1 to 3 months of a basic pay package as well as additional severance for each year of service to the company. Finally, an executive generally can expect to receive anywhere from 4 months to more than a year of pay as well as other bonuses and benefits.

Many people hear about thousands upon thousands of layoffs and tales of juicy severance packages. What many don't realize is that companies don't have to offer severance packages when they sever a relationship with employees. A company can simply downsize, lay off an employee, and say, "Pack your bags, we will escort you out the door, and as of right now, you no longer have a job or benefits." Some employees do, at the onset of their employment with a company, inquire about the position a company takes regarding severance packages and will negotiate a package for themselves should they be a future candidate for a reduction in force. A well-thought-out severance package tells a great deal about a company and how it views its employees. Savvy employees will see through the flaws, holes, and inconsistencies in a company's policy on severance.

It is important to communicate the specific components of a severance package when employees are laid off, including how pay is calculated, how many unused paid vacation days they have accrued, and the terms of benefits. Clarifying these issues for employees will not only make for an easier transition, but will demonstrate how valued employees are to the company. Enumerating these specifics will relieve many unresolved questions in the mind of severed employees.

DAMAGE CONTROL

After a company conducts a layoff, the fallout can be damaging to the corporate image. How will the community react? Will the company lose credibility? Its customers? What about suppliers? How does the company counteract negative publicity? Should it attempt to negate any bad aftershocks through good public relations, advertising, grass-roots efforts, and at what cost?

This tough problem requires a thoughtful response. Many companies are reluctant to do anything upfront and prefer to react after the fact becasue they're not sure of everyone's opinions. Other firms, however, are proactive and decide to deal with the problem head-on, approaching it with the right spin. Whether the company does nothing—as some would recommend—or takes action upfront, there are certain steps that should be followed.

Taking a Proactive Stance. Deciding to take action is the easy part. Figuring out exactly what to do is much harder. There are ways to spread the good word about a company. The thinking here is that outsiders will minimize the significance of the layoff if the company decides to share the news rather than have the news leaked or discovered after the fact. It also may negate any nasty rumors that may circulate if the news is kept a secret.

Those in charge of the media launch, whether internal staff or external consultants, should send out press releases to appropriate media—international, national, and regional, to wire services, industry associations, and trade magazines, newsletters, television and radio stations, and to any other appropriate sources, such as suppliers and customers, who will also have great concern about what's going on. The release should explain all the information that readers will want to know and focus on issues that might cause concern. Among these are:

- Why is the layoff needed?
- When will it happen?
- What will the effect be on company revenue, profits, new products, and services?
- How many employees will be cut now and will another cut be likely in a few months?
- What kind of severance will be offered? Will other services such as outplacement or counseling be available and for free?
- Will management change at all?
- What other repercussions will there be such as hiring freezes, pay cuts, or the elimination of overtime and perks?
- Will any offices or plants, domestic or overseas, have to be sold, liquidated, and closed?
- What is the morale of management and staff and what will be done to improve it?

The message should be short, succinct, and simple. It should be relevant and have some news value. No claims should be unsubstantiated.

At the same time the press releases are sent, management should be prepared to field questions with prepared answers. How this will be done should be planned far in advance through detailed media training with a public relations expert taking everyone through the paces, anticipating questions, explaining what should be told and not revealed, and identifying who in the company will handle what aspects of the layoff and which questions. Often a script can be prepared ahead of anticipated questions. The company's attorney may also want to be involved to approve what's said and written and what's not okay to divulge.

In most cases there will be a need for follow-up after press releases are sent. Management may decide to hold a press conference. The public and press will have questions about the future hiring and the effects of the layoff for weeks and months to come. How honest and forthcoming the company personnel are can help put the right spin on this down period in the company's history.

Taking a Reactive Stance. If the company decides not to share the news and word leaks out, the company will have to react—and again fast. However, it will now be doing so defensively. This route usually proves tougher because the press may dig more due to its supposition that there is more to conceal. The mood will become more combative, the questions more pointed, and the negative spin will be harder to turn around to a positive advantage.

In addition, the company's senior leadership will need to meet immediately, almost in a war room-type atmosphere. They will have to decide how to field phone calls, who will field them, and what the answers will be. They will probably also have to write an emergency press release to explain what's happening and why and send it over a newswire as well as make it accessible to reporters' e-mails and faxes and also to suppliers and customers.

Sometimes the damage can be contained, and the explanations, if detailed enough, will satisfy the public and the press. However, the tension will be much greater if any public relations work is done after bad news has leaked. It's a risk many companies prefer not to take.

KEEPING THE DOOR OPEN

Many people who have been laid off from their jobs have experienced some startling contrasts. One person described the experience as follows: "It was the most humiliating and demeaning experience of my life. I was notified by e-mail. Then security arrived at my door and escorted me from the building. I have nothing nice to say about the company, and you can be assured that I will do everything in my power to let everyone know what a heartless, deceitful company it is. I pray with all my strength that it will go under soon. This couldn't happen to a nicer company, could it?"

Contrast this with the reflection of a fiftysomething leaving one of America's most admired companies. "Sure, I would have liked to stay, but the company was going through an awful time. I cannot complain about the way I was treated. Management was very clear in reminding me how valued I am, and they acknowledged the contribution I had made to the company over the years. They also keep me in the family, in the sense that we stay in touch, and I have access to the employee clubs and the credit union. Almost every month, someone from the company calls to check in and see if they can be of any help."

Which of the two companies will be in a better position to recruit former employees once the business turns around? Of course, the second one. The biggest mistake to be made when laying off people is to act as if there will be no consequences once an employee exits. Companies often make the mistake of acting as if there is no need to be concerned with former employees once they are cut from the employee ranks. These are the companies that do not have a strategy regarding their former employees. They are focused only on those who have survived. That's a big mistake. The way in which a company separates, lays off, or fires people will have a direct impact on future performance as a company. The company has a lot at stake in keeping the door open to separated employees:

1. **The company's image as a desirable employer.** An image as an employer of choice or as one of America's best companies is difficult to earn and easy to lose. Companies like Eastman Kodak, Motorola, and IBM have taken decades to earn their reputation as family-friendly employers of choice. So when they experienced the first major layoffs in their histories in recent years, they had to take careful steps to protect their reputations. Each of these companies kept the door open as a major strategy.

2. **The company's ability to attract employees.** Would the employee laid off from the first company in the opening story accept an offer to return if there were a choice? In a turnaround companies compete for scarce talent. A bad separation experience not only poisons the waters for recruiting former employees, but the word can spread like the flu to all other candidates in the market. Companies risk their future when they make mistakes in separating people, which is why companies are so eager to do well and be included on lists such as "best companies to work for in America." These reputations are hard to come by.

3. **The company's ability to retain.** A botched separation speaks volumes to survivors as well. A common reaction characteristic of survivor syndrome is: "Wow. That could have been me! If they think so little of Ben, can you imagine what will happen to me when it's my turn?" In fact many managers will not have to worry about additional rounds of layoffs because people will seek to leave as soon as word about the layoffs gets out.

4. **The company's culture.** Nastiness can be contagious. It can infect a culture quickly, destroy morale, and lead to precipitous drops in productivity. It becomes a vicious circle that creates a self-fulfilling prophecy. The very positive values the company cultivated such as an optimistic outlook, high energy levels,

and risk taking are driven away by anger, resentment, protective behavior, passive aggression, poor quality, and an "I don't give a damn" attitude among survivors. The result can be further declines in productivity and profits, more rounds of layoffs, and ultimately, the demise of the organization.

Key Strategies for Keeping the Door Open. A smart company establishes a comprehensive strategy for keeping its door open. The experience of savvy companies dictates that four components make up this strategy. They consist of steps any company can and should take when separating employees, to maximize the future ability to attract and retain key talent.

1. **Treat people with honesty and dignity.** All companies are tempted to avoid difficult conversations and tough situations. But when they do, they may inadvertently be dishonest in their dealings with others and actually demean people. Hiding behind an e-mail and having security officers escort an employee past coworkers do not cut it. Employees deserve honesty and at least an explanation regarding the circumstances behind the separation. They deserve an honest assessment of their future with no false promises. They deserve dignity, an opportunity to finish what they have been doing and to talk with co-workers, if they choose.

2. **Provide furloughs.** Companies that are heavily invested in human capital have adopted furloughs as a strategy to keep open the door. Most furloughs maintain close connections with separated employees. It is much more intimate than a call back list. Managers keep monthly contact with the furloughed employee. Many furlough policies call for first refusal being granted as new positions and opportunities develop. A furlough sends a strong message: We care about you and want you back as soon as the opportunity exists.

3. **Offer assistance on separation.** Separation packages are critical to keeping the door open. The provision of placement services, assistance with career planning, and the like demonstrates that the company cares enough to take accountability for allaying some of the pain of a layoff.

4. **Maintain contacts with former employees.** Where feasible, companies should take steps to maintain contact with those they have separated. Examples include periodic social events and other organized means to maintain contact.

Keeping the door open will not happen spontaneously. It will only work if it is a deliberate strategy undertaken as part of the broader headcount solution. It will require accountability for actions and results on the part of all members of the organization to keep in touch with former staff on an ongoing basis.

SUMMARY

- There are intangible costs to reduce a work force. Failure to handle layoffs in a consistent and fair manner increases the odds that an employee will take legal action, bad-mouth the company, or pursue both routes.

- Layoffs done indiscriminately may also increase risks of inappropriate or illegal conduct such as inventory shrinkage, vandalism, theft of confidential information, industrial sabotage, or workplace violence.

- Legal red flags require additional due diligence. Managers need to take into account federal and state laws and regulations, so they need to be briefed far in advance.

- The company's survivors—those not fired—need to be listened to and supported to ensure the company can rebuild with them as part of a strong foundation for the future.

SAMPLE LETTERS TO COMPLY WITH WARN
SAMPLE LETTER TO ALL EMPLOYEES OF THE COMPANY
MEMORANDUM

TO: All ABC Company Employees

FROM: _____, President of ABC Company

DATE:

RE: Potential Closure of ABC Company

During the past several months, a general decline in our industry has impacted ABC Company both operationally and financially. All of us have worked hard to improve performance in the hope that we could turn ABC's financial problems around. However, most recently the situation has taken a turn for the worse. In late November and early December, many of our key vendors began cutting back credit, thus cutting back our general inventory. At the end of December, we lost three of our most experienced salespeople to competitors, whose combined business adds up to over X million dollars of annual sales, which is about 20 percent of our business. It is likely these salespeople will take almost all of that business to our competitors. Finally, two weeks ago, XYZ Company, our *only* supplier, announced that it will no longer provide us with inventory. The combination of these factors led us to reevaluate the direction ABC is currently taking as a company.

It was our initial hope to maintain ABC as a going concern and save the jobs of all employees. We looked at every avenue available to avoid shutting down, including additional financing. Also, with the goal of keeping ABC open, we have sought, and continue to actively seek, a prospective purchaser who would continue operations as is. However, after speaking with other companies in this field as recently as last Thursday, it is looking increasingly likely that the only purchasers interested will liquidate ABC, close down the company, and keep only the inventory.

We regret to inform you that there is a real possibility that ABC Company **[insert address of ABC]** must close within the next several weeks. This closing will result in the termination of employment for all ABC employees, and will be permanent. If nothing changes in terms of finding a purchaser for the company, we expect the first separation to occur by **[insert specific date]**. It is with this possibility in mind that we are issuing this notice in compliance with both the Federal WARN Act and the [State] Business Closing and the [State] Lay-off Act.

Please contact **[insert name and phone number of company official]** if you have any questions. Thank you for all of your hard work on behalf of ABC Company. We wish you well in all of your future endeavors.

SAMPLE NOTICE OF STATE DISLOCATED WORKERS UNIT, ISSUED PURSUANT TO WARN

[Date]
Dislocated Workers Unit
Department of Workforce Development
[City, State]

Re: Potential Closure of ABC Company

To Whom It May Concern,

It is with great regret that we inform you ABC Company is likely to discontinue operations within the next several weeks. ABC has confronted a series of financial problems within the last few months, including the loss of some key vendors and salespeople who have taken business with them as they left to work for our competitors. The company has explored many options with the hope of keeping ABC open and operating. We have investigated, without success, recapitalization and equity infusion. We have also actively sought, and continue to seek a purchaser who would keep operations as is. However, after speaking with other companies in our field as recently as Thursday, [**date**], it is looking increasingly likely that the only purchasers interested will liquidate ABC Company, close down the company, and keep only the inventory.

Thus, the employment of [**insert Number**] employees at the following location will likely end, effective beginning [**insert specific date**]:

ABC Company
Address

We expect this closure to be permanent. We have attached a list containing the names, addresses, and job titles of all affected employees

[**Attach list**]. If you need further information, you may contact [**insert name and phone number**].

Sincerely,

_____, CEO
ABC Company

SAMPLE LETTER TO LOCAL OFFICIAL

[Date]

The Honorable _____
City Hall
[Address]

Re: Potential Closure of ABC Company

Dear Mayor _____,

It is with great regret that we inform you that ABC Company is likely to discontinue operations within the next several weeks. ABC has confronted a series of financial problems within the last few months, including the loss of some key vendors and salespeople who have taken business with them as they left to work for our competitors. The company has explored many options with the hope of keeping ABC open and operating. We have investigated, without success, recapitalization and equity infusion. We have also actively sought, and continue to seek, a purchaser who would keep operations as is. However, after speaking with other companies in our field as recently as of [**date**], it is looking increasingly likely that the only purchasers interested will liquidate ABC, close down the company, and keep only the inventory.

Thus, the employment of [**insert Number**] employees at the following location will likely end, effective beginning [**insert specific date**]:

ABC Company
Address

We expect this closure to be permanent. We have attached a list containing the names, addresses, and job titles of all affected employees [**attach list**]. If you need further information, you may contact [**insert name and phone number**].

Sincerely,

_____, CEO
ABC Company

SAMPLE LETTER TO UNION REPRESENTATIVE OF THE AFFECTED EMPLOYEES

[Date]
Mr. _____
President
Local No.
International Union of _____
[Address]
Re: Immediate layoffs at ABC Company

Dear **[insert name of president of Local No.]**,

It is with regret that I inform you that ABC Company will layoff a significant number of employees at the end of business today. ABC is confronting significant, serious financial issues which affect our ability to conduct various operations on a continuing basis. The company has engaged in negotiations with its principal customers and lender to seek needed financial accommodations. However this week it became apparent that the company would not be able to obtain financial accommodations sufficient to permit it to continue operations at current levels. Therefore, the employment of **[insert number]** employees at XYZ, a division of ABC Company, **[insert address]** will end effective today, **[date]**.

We expect this layoff to be indefinite. ABC will follow bumping procedures in accordance with Article __ of the collective bargaining agreement with Local No. ___.

A list of the affected bargaining unit employees is attached and includes each employee's address and job title. If you need further information, you may contact **[name]**, in the company's Human Resources Department, **[phone number]**.

Sincerely,

_____
ABC Company
by its CEO

CHAPTER 10

Step 7: Help Survivors Cope and Get Back to Business

KEY PRINCIPLES

- Companies that rebound successfully have mastered the Headcount Solution. They have planned for a turnaround that provides for maximizing human capital.

- Rebuilding the work force requires an optimistic view of the future and a way to harness the skills and competencies of the existing remaining work force.

REBUILDING THE WORK FORCE

Companies will be shocked and shaken by cost cutting and reductions in force, but there are steps to take to regain momentum and rebuild. After conducting cost-cutting measures, here are the ways to take control of the situation and turn the corner to recovery.

1. Do not Forget the Needs of the Survivors. There is a need to address the anxieties of those who survive a layoff, especially if there is more than one round of cost cutting. Those left behind are typically ambivalent. There is postlayoff guilt. They think, "Why me? Why did someone who was here 20 years get laid off and I've only been here 5 years and get to stay?" They are relieved to have a job but upset because those they worked with are gone and may resent them. Furthermore, they may have to assume other tasks. And they might be uncomfortable with the fact that they could be the next to get fired. They may have the feeling of needing to look over their shoulders or await their pink slips, which makes their daily hard work almost impossible.

Companies should work with the survivors and offer them an outlet to express their feelings, whether that involves giving them access to a counselor or supervisors to validate that their anxiety is perfectly normal.

Most important, the company should not make any guarantees. Do not say, "This won't happen to you." Rather, be honest with staff about the company finances and status and the reason the layoffs had to be done in the first place. Management should convey to the survivors this message: "We're glad you are still with the company. We hope we can all do what needs to be done to get the company back on strong financial ground." Make employees feel like partners in that goal. Also make clear to survivors the value of their contribution to the company's financial success. Assure them that the company will do its best to avoid additional layoffs.

2. Concentrate on Rebuilding Employee Loyalty and Morale and Rewarding Employee Performance.

Companies that follow the Headcount Solution—even if all options are exhausted and employees must eventually be laid off—have far improved employee morale in the short term during troubled times. Companies taking this path have found that as conditions improve, their people are more loyal, feel better protected, and will spread a good word to others about the firm.

Consider the following example of a company that has a guaranteed employment policy for those who have been with the company for 3 years on a full-time basis. This policy at Lincoln Electric in Cleveland, Ohio, a corporation of 7000 employees worldwide, does not preclude the fact that an employee might be reassigned to a different job or that the pay scale for the job might change. But the employee will not be terminated. In fact, in the U.S. operation, there has not been a single layoff since 1948. In the early to mid-1980s, when production dropped, instead of cutting the work force, it took those on the shop floor, put suits and ties on them, and placed them in sales positions. By doing so these "salespeople" developed a new customer base. When work picked up and people went back to their former jobs, some opted to stay in sales. Employees were allowed to demonstrate new, perhaps unknown, skill sets and interests. Additionally, these employees needed no training because they were already familiar with the company, its mission, goals, and values.

But what about companies that conduct layoffs? Building morale is more difficult, but following are a few simple guidelines that will make it easier:

- **Continue to communicate.** Just because the crisis is over, managers should not stop the process that has been put into place. Once employees are "in the loop," it makes sense to keep the information flowing as well as employee involvement and suggestions. Employees can help out in good times as well as bad.

- **Put the next round of incentives in place.** Often companies return to a more discretionary bonus and incentive program after the crisis has been resolved. The type of turnaround bonus described in Chapter 3 works for taking performance to new levels as well as in a turnaround situation.

- **Reward the best performers.** When the merit budget is tight, there is a concentrated effort to reward key top performers. When conditions improve, the best performers should not be forgotten. Room should be made to provide merit compensation and recognition for them.

3. Be Creative with Employee Work Assignments. Emphasize new opportunities that have the potential for long-term profitable growth. Focus on the company's strengths and build them up with human capital. Use creativity and energy to look to the future in the following ways:

- **Take the opportunity to cross-train employees.** Allow employees new opportunities to learn and test their skills. Train them and the company will gain an employee with existing intellectual knowledge of the company that does not exist in a new hire. It's tough to lose certain employees, and it is important to retain the knowledge and experience base. (See Chapter 5.) To do so might mean taking those who were underemployed and putting them in another department. For example, put accounting people in engineering or out on the road in jobs not too far afield from their original skills. This enables them to see a different perspective of the business. Cross-training also builds bridges; it develops relationships and those relationships tend to remain intact.

- **Shift the focus to results.** Alternative work arrangements shift from paying people for their time at a desk to paying for what is produced. One East Coast company cut back on hours and instituted telecommuting. It created a void in how the company usually managed people. The issue became trusting what wasn't in the field of vision of the manager. But leadership learned that employees don't have to be visible or work a traditional 40-hour work week to accomplish what needs to be done. They can do so on their own if properly motivated.

- **Jump-start projects.** Put creative people in teams to tackle a product or new service that the company could develop or improve. Too often a company focuses only on what it has done in the past in its market segment. Assign staff to look for new opportunities to generate income. It could prove valuable. In the best case scenario, if just one project catches on, it could be the next margin opportunity for the company.

- **Lead with optimism.** Senior leadership should balance current problems against the future for the company and anticipate a successful turnaround.

4. Create Ways to Keep Laid-off Employees Connected to the Company.
Try to bring back those laid off as soon as possible. When the firm turns around financially, it will have an improved, full staff of people with new skill sets to choose from instead of a skeleton staff.

Massive layoffs may translate to a loss of future sales if demand ramps up quickly and the firm cannot find sufficient personnel fast enough to meet demand. Using layoffs as a first resort when the economy dips may diminish the firm's market position and status as a market leader as well as its competitive position in the future.

It's up to senior leadership to keep the environment positive after a layoff. They need to remain upbeat for those who are leaving and those who are left. A positive or negative attitude can quickly become contagious, so they must set the right mood. Business and life go on, even in tough times.

CREATIVE WAYS TO REWARD THE SURVIVORS

The company may not have extra funds to offer its surviving troops and it doesn't have great news to share, but it still has opportunities and challenges in its future. These include a distinct culture, active leadership, hardworking staff, and if it does its homework, a host of ways to say, "We care" and "We want you to remain."

This is more critical than ever when people are not at the top of their game. They're shell-shocked by what's occurred; they're sad and angry. Senior leadership and managers should try to motivate staff to stay with the company and give their best as individuals, teams, and part of the whole company. The approaches recommended here should also augment a targeted cash incentive plan, as outlined in Chapter 3, if at all possible.

There are numerous ways to reward and motivate creatively as shown in Table 10-1. It begins with emphasizing a quality work environment and includes a company culture, recognition of employees

Table 10-1   Creative Ways to Motivate and Reward Your Best People

A Quality Work Environment			
Culture	**Recognition**	**Flexibility**	**The Work Itself**
Rebuild on company values	Emphasize formal and informal recognition for work accomplishments	Look for ways to ease the greater work burden on the survivors	Look to enhance the inherent value you place on the survivors

for their contributions, flexibility on the part of the company, and the work itself. These all contribute to a sense of value and mutual commitment between employers and employees.

CULTURE

Culture refers to an organization's shared values. The elements include human values such as caring, concern, achievement, informality, and commitment. An organization's true culture is not what is said in its mission statement, but what is played out daily in the way people act toward one another and the company. The aftermath of a layoff presents an excellent opportunity for senior leadership to ask the important questions: "What kind of culture will best serve us, and how do we get there from here?"

The best companies to work for consistently are differentiated by how much confidence their employees have in the company, its shared values, the challenge of the work, and its reputation in its industry. No matter how large or small, a company's culture develops over time from actual behavior. Management needs to provide leadership by "walking the talk" and creating a culture that instills commitment and mutual respect. Rebuilding starts one step at a time. For example, one manager intended for years to delegate more and allow his staff a wider berth in planning its work and meeting assignment deadlines. Regrouping after a layoff provided an excellent opportunity for him to address the issue and make some significant changes in expectations regarding work style and completed tasks.

RECOGNITION

This may be among the least understood and least utilized rewards. It consists of positive feedback, reaction to achievements, tangible reinforcement through additional feedback, and on occasion something as simple as a "thank you."

According to decades of management research, feedback may be the single most important reward to most employees. The lack of feedback in turn may be the single most punishing experience on a job.

To start, a manager can reward someone through recognition on a daily, informal basis. Good managers should be on the lookout for examples of outstanding individual and group achievement. They should be told in words or in writing (a thank you note) when they've hit a home run—or even reached first base. Employees, too, should be told to look for examples of recognizing their colleagues and expressing it. For example, Corning Inc. has employee kiosks located throughout each of its units. Slips of paper are provided for an employee to write down examples of excellent accomplishments and reward fellow employees or teams on the spot.

Some companies develop more formal recognition programs such as awards for specific individual or team achievements or customer service awards. Although a recovery may not be the best time for designing and implementing such a system from scratch, it is a good time to review current recognition programs in place and renew or add to them.

FLEXIBILITY

Anyone who employs technology-oriented employees learns that flexibility and informality are key facets of interest to them on their jobs. For example, Motorola conducted research on its own employees and found flexibility and informality to be among the most important drivers of employee satisfaction. Other similar components of satisfaction included access to key technical people and respect for individual differences. This type of flexibility is not expensive to implement. Managers must closely examine their own practices to determine the concerns and issues of the survivors, who may have greater workloads than before the layoff.

One manager thought about how to structure work for a group of technical programmers who had survived a layoff. Clearly, fewer would have to pick up the work of what had been a larger team. The following issues occurred to her as she thought about how to change their job descriptions:

1. "We better get nonessential work out of here. We need to look closely at our processes and limit ourselves to critical path activities."

2. "We can work more efficiently if we do away with barriers created by our current functional job descriptions. With some cross-training, we should be more flexible in conducting projects. Maybe we can identify some shared accountabilities that will move work faster with the same heads."

3. "Perhaps I should not manage each person's time so closely. I could set time limits, project expectations, and allow the team to organize its time on its own. We could carve out time for people to devote to projects of special interest to them."

After laying out these thoughts, she asked for some reaction. She found an untapped well of ideas and enthusiasm that created a win/win situation. Team members were able to structure their personal activities in a more flexible fashion, which also allowed employees to pursue individual interests, yet the overall work of the department improved in quality and productivity.

THE WORK ITSELF

The single most important source of motivation—what really turns on an employee—is work. One of life's most punishing circumstances is to work at a boring job, day after day, whereas one of life's greatest gifts involves a challenging, fulfilling job experience, not necessarily every day but often enough.

The most powerful tool at a manager's disposal to reenergize and motivate survivors is to reenergize their workloads positively. Five steps can help:

1. Make sure that a job has variety. Nothing is duller than doing a limited set of activities daily. Look for ways to broaden and deepen accountabilities on the job and make it more interesting.

2. Give employees more autonomy. Empower them. Put them in charge of more decisions. Set longer term goals; allow them freedom to act. Manage results.

3. Give employees important assignments. Minimize or eliminate trivia. Make sure employees have accountabilities that relate directly to their department and organization's central mission and process.

4. Give employees visibility for what they do. Let employees get face time with other units and with customers. Make sure that others in the organization understand what each employee does and why it is important to the company's success. Make the employees' contributions visible to the organization and customers.

5. Provide consistent feedback. The single most powerful reward, again, is information that explains how an employee is doing and what the person can do to improve.

GETTING BACK TO BUSINESS

A business crisis challenges the abilities of every leader. The fear created by uncertainty can cloud decisions and paralyze even the savviest managers. A wrong move, such as massive layoffs before alternatives are considered, can dramatically affect how well a business survives the crisis. It may also position it poorly for recovery and spur qualified employees to leave.

Companies that survive and rebound have learned to plan for their future. They assess their current employees' skill sets, determine what skills will be required in the future, and create special ways to cut costs before laying off staff. They have learned that sustainable growth with the right people on board is critical to restore profitability rather than temporarily save by cutting heads—and jobs.

Witness this example. Grace Perry, an executive with Lathem Time of Atlanta, an 80-year-old, 150-employee family business that manufactures and designs timekeeping products, saw firsthand the dramatic impact of an economic downturn on the business. Perry said that to cut employees across the board would have hurt the company more than it would help.

Yet the firm found it mandatory to cut costs to stay in business. Here's what Lathem did, and it worked. It showed employees first that it was willing to try everything possible to avoid layoffs. The average employee had been on board 15 years. But to cut costs without layoffs became more of a challenge. The company tried something novel. It cut labor costs, not heads, by asking employees to accept a reduction in work hours.

Employees were supportive. They agreed to take a salary reduction and work 36-hour weeks or four 9 hour days plus a half-day on Fridays if needed. This benefited both sides—labor and management. The company saved money, was more in control of its costs, and did not lose anything in terms of productivity. In fact this streamlined the operation. Furthermore, employees had longer weekends, which meant they were more rested and focused on their workdays.

Interestingly, Perry said that the move provided residual benefits. Managers were forced to stay on their toes and look at how individuals worked in their teams. Work processes were changed, and it forced Lathem to take a look at what it was doing. Moreover, the firm did not have to pay for overtime.

This was not enough, however. To reduce costs more, the company resorted to two small rounds of layoffs that involved about 20 employees. In addition, some employees, who were close to retirement, left of their own volition. Management looked at each area and saw where it could afford to make cuts. Seniority was not the main strategy; rather, it was the importance of the job. Management looked at the products, the costs to produce them, and where it could afford to let one person go in each area.

This approach proved successful. Perry noted that if the company had not tried to cut costs early on the way it did, it would have lost money. This would have ultimately resulted in larger layoffs. As it turned out, the company recovered. Furthermore, employees were an integral part of arriving at a solution. They were communicated with frequently, were made aware of the difficult situation the company faced, and were dealt with in a straightforward, honest manner.

Such stories abound throughout corporate America as examples of companies that have learned to understand the value of alternatives to layoffs.

The desire and opportunity to work are the fuel for an effective organization. After implementing the Headcount Solution, an organization will still be facing many business challenges, but the job will be made easier with a work force that has been preserved through a crisis, held together, and has become stronger as a result. The painful journey through a business crisis lays the foundation for taking advantage of new opportunities and new successes that lie in the future.

SUMMARY

- Senior leadership needs to parlay a negative into a positive. Leadership should engage the talents and energy of employees to turn the corner and move forward.

- Leadership needs to consider survivors' needs. Employees need reassurance and recognition for their importance. They hold the reputation and future of the company in their hands.

- The Headcount Solution is designed to save the organization from a business crisis and lay the foundation for pursuing new business opportunities and new growth.

Sample Employment Termination Agreement for an Individual 40 Years of Age or Older

This Agreement can be modified for Early Retirement by substituting Early Retirement benefits for Separation Pay, inserting the date of Early Retirement, and specifying that the Early Retirement is voluntary.

SEPARATION AGREEMENT
AND GENERAL RELEASE

ABC Company ("ABC") and _____("Employee") agree as follows:

1. In consideration for Employee signing this Agreement and Release, ABC has agreed to pay Employee an additional _____ of salary ($_____, less deductions required by law) as "Separation Pay."

2 GENERAL RELEASE—In return for the consideration set forth above, Employee agrees not to sue or file any action, claim or lawsuit against ABC, agrees not to pursue, seek to recover or recover any alleged damages, seek to obtain or obtain any other form of relief or remedy with respect to, and will take action to cause the dismissal or withdrawal of, any lawsuit, action, claim or charge against ABC, and Employee agrees to waive all claims and release and forever discharge ABC, its officers, directors, shareholders, partners and employees from any and all claims, demands, actions, causes of action or liabilities for compensatory damages or any other relief or remedy, and obligations of any kind or nature what-soever, whether known or unknown, fixed or contingent, liquidated or unliquidated, and whether arising from tort, statute, or contract, including, but not limited to, any claims arising under or pursuant to Title VII of the Civil Rights Act of 1964, as amended, the Civil Rights Act of 1991, the Civil Rights Act of 1866, as amended, the Americans With Disabilities Act, the Rehabilitation Act, the Family and Medical Leave Act, the Occupational Safety &

Health Act, the Employee Retirement Income Security Act of 1974, as amended, the Age Discrimination in Employment Act, Executive Orders 11246 and 11375, the Worker Adjustment and Retraining Notification Act, the Fair Labor Standards Act, any other federal, state, city, county, municipal, or local governmental unit statute, rule, regulation, ordinance or order, any claim for future consideration for employment with ABC, any claims for attorneys' fees and costs and any employment rights or entitlement law, and any claims for wrongful discharge, intentional infliction of emotional distress, defamation, libel or slander, payment of wages, outrageous behavior, breach of contract or any duty allegedly owed to Employee, and any other theory of recovery. It is the intention of the parties to make this release as broad and as general as the law permits.

3. This Release may not be introduced in any legal or administrative proceeding, except one concerning a breach of this Release.

4. Employee agrees to maintain **confidentiality** regarding the terms of this Release. Employee may disclose information regarding the terms of this Release to her spouse, accountant, lawyer and financial advisor, provided that such individuals shall first agree to maintain confidentiality regarding the terms disclosed to them.

5. Employee is advised to consult with an attorney, at Employee's own expense, <u>prior</u> to signing this Release.

6. Employee acknowledges that Employee has fully read this Release, understands the contents of this Release, and agrees to its terms and conditions of Employee's own free will, knowingly and voluntarily, and without any duress or coercion.

7. Employee understands that this is a **final general release**, and that Employee can make no further claims against ABC concerning her employment and/or with respect to the matters referred to herein. Employee also agrees that Employee will fully waive

receiving any damages or other relief as a result of any lawsuit, grievance, charge or claim that may be brought on Employee's behalf and arising out of Employee's employment with ABC, or Employee's separation from employment with ABC. Employee does not release rights that may arise after the signing of this agreement.

8. Employee acknowledges that Employee is receiving adequate consideration (that is in addition to what Employee is entitled to) for signing this Release.

9. Employee has had a period of up to <u>twenty-one (21) days</u> to consider whether to accept and sign this Release.

10. Employee will have <u>seven (7) days</u> from the date Employee signs this Release to revoke Employee's acceptance of this Release.

11. If any provision of this Release is judicially held to be invalid, unenforceable or void, such holding shall not have the effect of invalidating or voiding the remainder of this Release, provided that the remaining provisions provide for the realization of the principal legal rights and benefits afforded by this Release.

12. This Release constitutes the complete understanding between Employee and ABC that supercedes all prior agreements and understandings between Employee and ABC. No other promises or agreements will be binding unless signed by Employee and ABC.

ABC Company   Employee

By:_____   _____

_____, 2003 _____, 2003

Sample Employment Termination Agreement to Be Used for More Than One Individual 40 Years of Age or Older

This Agreement can be modified for Early Retirement benefits by substituting Early Retirement for Separation Pay, inserting the date of Early Retirement and specifying that the Early Retirement is voluntary.

SEPARATION AGREEMENT
AND GENERAL RELEASE

ABC Company ("ABC") and _____ ("Employee") agree as follows:

1. In consideration for Employee signing this Agreement and Release, ABC has agreed to pay Employee an additional _____ of salary ($_____, less deductions required by law) as "Separation Pay."

2. <u>GENERAL RELEASE</u>—In return for the consideration set forth above, Employee agrees not to sue or file any action, claim or lawsuit against ABC, agrees not to pursue, seek to recover or recover any alleged damages, seek to obtain or obtain any other form of relief or remedy with respect to, and will take action to cause the dismissal or withdrawal of, any lawsuit, action, claim or charge against ABC, and Employee agrees to waive all claims and release and forever discharge ABC, its officers, directors, shareholders, partners and employees from any and all claims, demands, actions, causes of action or liabilities for compensatory damages or any other relief or remedy, and obligations of any kind or nature whatsoever, whether known or unknown, fixed or contingent, liquidated or unliquidated, and whether arising from tort, statute, or contract, including, but not limited to, any claims arising under or pursuant to Title VII of the Civil Rights Act of 1964, as amended, the Civil Rights Act of 1991, the Civil Rights Act of 1866, as amended, the Americans With Disabilities Act, the Rehabilitation Act, the Family and Medical Leave Act, the Occupational Safety & Health Act, the Employee Retirement Income Security Act of 1974, as amended, the Age Discrimination in

Employment Act, Executive Orders 11246 and 11375, the Worker Adjustment and Retraining Notification Act, the Fair Labor Standards Act, any other federal, state, city, county, municipal, or local governmental unit statute, rule, regulation, ordinance or order, any claim for future consideration for employment with ABC, any claims for attorneys' fees and costs and any employment rights or entitlement law, and any claims for wrongful discharge, intentional infliction of emotional distress, defamation, libel or slander, payment of wages, outrageous behavior, breach of contract or any duty allegedly owed to Employee, and any other theory of recovery. It is the intention of the parties to make this release as broad and as general as the law permits.

3. This Release may not be introduced in any legal or administrative proceeding, except one concerning a breach of this Release.

4. Employee agrees to maintain **confidentiality** regarding the terms of this Release. Employee may disclose information regarding the terms of this Release to her spouse, accountant, lawyer and financial advisor, provided that such individuals shall first agree to maintain confidentiality regarding the terms disclosed to them.

5. Employee is advised to consult with an attorney, at Employee's own expense, <u>prior</u> to signing this release.

6. Employee acknowledges that Employee has fully read this Release, understands the contents of this Release, and agrees to its terms and conditions of Employee's own free will, knowingly and voluntarily, and without any duress or coercion.

7. Employee understands that this is a **final general release**, and that Employee can make no further claims against ABC concerning her employment and/or with respect to the matters referred to herein. Employee also agrees that Employee will fully waive receiving any damages or other relief as a result of any lawsuit, grievance, charge or claim that may be brought on Employee's

behalf and arising out of Employee's employment with ABC, or Employee's separation from employment with ABC. Employee does not release rights that may arise after signing this agreement.

8. Employee acknowledges that Employee is receiving adequate consideration (that is in addition to what Employee is entitled to) for signing this Release.

9. Employee has had a period of up to <u>forty-five (45) days</u> to consider whether to accept and sign this Release. Pursuant to section 626(f)(1)(H) of the ADEA, ABC has provided disclosure in Attachment A of this Agreement*, concerning the availability of this severance package to other employees.

10. Employee will have <u>seven (7) days</u> from the date Employee signs this Release to revoke Employee's acceptance of this Release.

11. If any provision of this Release is judicially held to be invalid, unenforceable or void, such holding shall not have the effect of invalidating or voiding the remainder of this Release, provided that the remaining provisions provide for the realization of the principal legal rights and benefits afforded by this Release.

12. This Release constitutes the complete understanding between Employee and ABC. No other promises or Releases will be binding unless signed by Employee and ABC.

ABC Company   Employee

By:_____   _____

_____, 2003   _____, 2003

*If a group of employees is terminated, federal law requires that the employer must also inform the terminated employees of all individuals covered by this exit program, eligibility factors of this program, time limits applicable to this program, job titles and ages of all individuals eligible or selected for this program, and the ages of all individuals in the same job classification or organizational unit who are eligible or selected for this program.

Sample Speech: Announcing a Company Crisis

(Round 1 of Cost Cutting)

Good morning. For those who I've not had the opportunity to meet personally, my name is _____, _____'s (Company Name) president and chief operating officer. I come to you today with news about a difficult challenge our company will face over the next several weeks. It is one that will test us, yet one in which I am confident we will prevail and emerge a winner.

Our company faces a crisis that affects everyone in our industry. We have come through the fourth straight quarter of declining sales and profits. This last quarter we experienced a $25 million loss—one that we cannot afford to repeat. Your senior executives and the board know that our core strengths remain strong, that we can weather this downturn, and that we will emerge with a strong competitive advantage. But we won't survive to see that day if our costs keep mounting. We must take action now and that is why I have come to talk to you.

A $25 MILLION PROBLEM

We have a $25 million dollar problem. Our losses have been mounting and if we are going to survive, we must find ways to remove $25 million in costs as quickly as we possibly can. On the other hand we need to be smart about it. We cannot afford to lose the very talent we will need to survive this period in our company's history and to fight into the future.

Your senior executives, the board, and I have wrestled with the $25 million problem for several weeks now and have a game plan. I want to describe this plan to you, tell you how it will impact you, and answer any questions you will have about it. We have set two primary objectives for this plan:

1. Save the company and
2. Save jobs

I can't guarantee this morning that there will be no job loss. In fact there is a high probability that we will have to cut some jobs in the coming weeks. But I can promise you that I will do everything in my power to prevent job losses, and I think my past record demonstrates my honesty and credibility. We will take every step possible to cut costs before we are forced to cut jobs.

OUR GAME PLAN

Remember that I said we must get costs out, *yet we realize the importance of holding onto our valued employees.* That means cutting costs and saving jobs at the same time. That sounds like an oxymoron, doesn't it? Yes, but I am confident that we have a plan—a solution to the problem—that allows us to remove costs and minimize the impact on jobs here.

Here's our plan. We will attack the $25 million in three rounds.

ROUND 1: COST CUTTING

We will aggressively take all unnecessary, noncritical costs out of the company. We will look for any costs that can be cut without compromising our core business activities and without having to lay off employees.

I've asked a task force of top-level managers to identify immediate costs we can cut and they have reported back to me. Today, I am announcing that we are suspending bonuses for all employees (including myself and the senior staff) this year. In addition, we are cutting the salary increase budget for next year by one-half. These two actions alone will reduce our losses by $5 million. That means we have $20 million to go.

Next I am directing all department heads to find ways of cutting nonessential costs within their units. I am asking them to involve you in this process. The goal is to get as much cost out as possible without compromising our core businesses and without cutting jobs.

If we can get all costs out in this round, we'll be done. To be very honest with you, however, I don't believe we will be that lucky. That's why I want to prepare you this morning for two more rounds that are likely. Unfortunately, they are rounds that will affect people.

ROUND 2: ALTERNATIVE WORK ARRANGEMENTS

Before we lay anybody off, I have instructed all department heads to get creative about how we employ people. Right now, almost everyone who works for (Company) occupies a full-time job with full benefits, and that's the way we'd like it to stay. But what if we can't do this? Are there any alternatives that might not involve full employment, yet avoid a layoff? I've asked the human resources department to advise a task force of senior managers on this issue. Their mission is to find other ways such as job sharing, temporary assignments, and the like that might be available to us. I will talk more about these alternatives in our next meeting, once the task force gets back to me. That meeting is scheduled in 2 weeks.

ROUND 3: LAYOFFS

I wish I could stand in front of you this morning and guarantee that there will be no layoffs. I would be lying, however, and I have always committed myself to being bone honest with you. There remains the possibility that we will not be able to get all of the $25 million in costs out in Rounds 1 and 2. If this is the case, we will have to resort to limited layoffs. I do commit, again, to you that we will take every step possible to limit or even do away with the need for layoffs. But to be frank, they remain a high probability at this point.

HOW WILL THIS AFFECT ME?

You have every right and should ask, "How will this affect me?" First, let me answer that we are all members of the same family here, and we will all feel the pain over the next several weeks. We're all going to be living with some degree of uncertainty about our company, our jobs, and our future. In addition, some of the first-round cuts may be uncomfortable. A lower raise this year may well cut into important family plans that you all have already made such as a wedding or family vacation or remodeling.

WHAT AM I ASKING OF YOU?

Whether we succeed depends on you personally. I am asking a lot of you this morning. Specifically, I am asking you to do the following:

1. Keep your confidence in our company and our ability to succeed in the future. I assure you that in spite of this quarter's losses we remain a healthy company at the core, and we have what it takes to succeed.

2. Get up each morning and think about our $25 million problem. Ask yourself: "What can I do, what can my team do, what can the company do to get unnecessary costs out?"

3. Share your ideas with coworkers and managers.

4. Don't sit back and wait. Join your department's efforts to identify cost-cutting opportunities.

5. Most important, don't forget your work in all of this. I trust all of you will be diligent about conducting your work and keeping the company on track.

I love this company and hope you will join me in a commitment to persevere in these difficult times. Together, I am confident that we will come out of this with a company we can be proud of and which will survive.

Thank you for your attention. Let me now answer any questions you might have.

Sample Speech: Announcing Alternative Work Arrangements

(Round 2 of Cost Cutting)

Good morning. Thank you for attending this morning. We met 2 weeks ago to discuss the strategy the company is following to remove $25 million in costs from our operations. In that meeting I announced the first of three rounds in this effort, finding ways to remove costs without impairing our core business operations and influencing employment. We have completed that round, and I am happy to announce that we have found ways to remove $10 million of the $25 million that the company must remove to regain profitability. Suspending bonuses and cutting raises in half alone saved us $5 million, and we did not have to cut any jobs or cut into base salaries.

We still have $15 million to go, and the purpose of today's meeting is to describe the second round in our efforts, the introduction of alternative work arrangements. Over the last 2 weeks, I have asked a task force of senior managers, assisted by the HR department, to explore ways we can cut employment costs while still retaining people, at least on a part-time basis. The idea is to find alternatives to full-time employment that will get compensation costs down, while avoiding layoffs. They have found three creative alternative arrangements that will be feasible in our situation. They are:

1. **Job/skill sharing.** The first is called job or skill sharing. Under this arrangement two people will go back to part-time work and share a single job. The downside is that you earn only part of your normal salary. The upside is you retain at least part of your job and income, and you retain full benefits (including health insurance).

2. **Contracting.** The second way is contracting, an arrangement under which you change from being an employee to being a contractor to the company. In effect you go into your own business, and we become your customer. The downside is that you lose employment status (and the benefits). The upside is that you retain income, accomplished through

the professional fees charged to us for your services. You become responsible for paying your own benefits and paying your own income taxes. The company will also extend your health benefits for 2 months and, under the COBRA regulations, you can purchase the company's health plan for up to 18 months after that. You may want to consider other alternatives since COBRA is expensive. If you have a spouse, see if you can be covered under his or her plan or consider other options for individuals.

I hope that some of you who take these routes truly become successful entrepreneurs and that the company will be the first of many new clients you serve. We know we run the risk that you find the contracting situation very desirable, and if we might want to rehire you in the future you may not wish to come back.

3. **Special assignments.** The third alternative we are considering is to take some people whose jobs have been cut and keep them either as full- or part-time on special assignments. Many of you have specialized skills that we can apply to specific projects. We can't guarantee employment long term, but we can use your talents on a project-by-project basis. The upside is that you retain all or part of your employment status with us. The downside is that there is no guarantee of continued employment after the project is finished.

HOW WILL THIS AFFECT ME?

Let me now shift to what's going to happen over the next 2 weeks and how this will affect you. I am asking each department head to create a headcount plan for his or her department over the next week. Each of them will have a goal to achieve in reducing employment costs beyond the $10 million we have saved in Round 1.

Each department head will conduct a human capital analysis. In this analysis he or she will inventory the mission-critical skills necessary to maintain our effective operations. I will be asking them to evaluate everyone in the department with respect to these skills. Your department head will decide who will remain in full employment status and who will be offered one of the alternative work arrangements I have just mentioned. I will be asking the department heads to be making their decisions based primarily on a consideration of who has the critical skills we need most. They will also rely, secondarily, on considerations of relative performance merit and experience with the company and the department. I assure you that we will take every step possible to make sure that this difficult process occurs in a fair and consistent fashion and avoids favoritism of any kind.

I understand that it's not an easy process. Nobody likes to be evaluated, especially under the gun. Nobody likes this type of stress and pressure, least of all me and your managers. But it's a necessary process, and your department heads will be biting the bullet to make these choices. I ask each department head to consult with your direct reports in this process. I urge each of you to make your preferences known to your superiors. Finally, I ask each department head to accommodate preferences as much as possible.

I would like to believe that we could be done after this round and that we can avoid layoffs. Maybe that will happen. But we can't count on it now. I will be meeting with you in 2 weeks to share the results of Round 2 with you.

Let me take this opportunity to thank each and every one of you for your understanding and support during this difficult time. Your company needs you and we need each other more than ever.

Thank you. May I or anyone else who is part of senior management answer any questions? Don't be shy. Now is the time for questions and a healthy dialogue.

Sample Speech: Layoff Announcement

(Round 3 of Cost Cutting)

Good morning. Thank you for attending this morning. This is our third meeting to discuss our efforts to remove $25 million in costs so that we may save our company. We have completed two rounds of cost cutting.

In Round 1 we were able to remove $10 million in costs, leaving us with $15 million more to cut. In Round 2 we explored ways to use alternatives such as job sharing, contracting, and temporary assignments to pare costs further. The results are in, and we have reduced our costs by another $10.3 million. I want to take this opportunity to thank those employees who have agreed to these arrangements and for their part in helping us.

I said at the first meeting that I would always be honest with you. I added that I would prefer to have no layoffs, but there was a high probability these would have to occur. Unfortunately, I was correct in that prediction. We still have almost $4.7 million in costs that must come out. Our only alternative now is to reduce our employment by approximately 94 positions during the next week. We have identified those who will be asked to depart through the process of skill assessment that I described in our last meeting. The process has been fair, and it has taken each individual employee into account.

Let's take a minute to reflect on what has happened and what we have accomplished over the last few weeks. We have to remove $25 million from our operating costs. It is a step that must be done to save the company. We have tried to act as wisely as possible in doing so, first by exploring ways to cut costs without influencing employment and then by finding alternatives to full employment that would minimize the impact of a layoff. How well have we done? Let me share numbers with you.

If we had gone straight to a layoff, we would have had to cut our work force by 500 people. That represents about one-third of our total employment.

But we did the smart thing. In Round 1 we looked for costs to cut without a layoff. In Round 2 we introduced alternative work arrangements. Those actions allowed us to cut the potential layoff from 500 jobs to only 94 jobs. I hope you will agree with me that it was worth it!

Clearly, this is not good news for those of you who will be laid off. I know there is nothing we can do to make up this loss to you. I commit, however, to acting with the greatest dignity and respect in conducting this process. Specifically, I have directed senior managers to provide the following:

1. The process will be handled personally. There will be no anonymous or generic letters or e-mails.

2. Everyone laid off will be provided a financial severance package based on tenure with the company and level in the organization.

3. Everyone laid off will be provided continuation of benefits (commensurate with severance). You will also be eligible to purchase 18 months of health insurance at the company's rate under the federal COBRA law.

4. Everyone laid off will be provided outplacement services. We have retained XYZ Company to provide you office space, office services, counseling, interviewing practice, and résumé preparation for a thorough job search.

5. We are not going to forget you after you leave. We are going to take the following steps to keep the door open:

   a. We will include you on the invitation list for all company events, reunions, and picnics.

   b. You will retain your membership in the company health facilities and are welcome to use them any time, though for a fee once you leave.

    c.   You will be among the first considered for jobs when and if we can hire again.

Let me close by thanking all of you for your valiant efforts and contributions to the company over the last several weeks, months, and farther back—years. You have indeed saved our company. I am convinced that we will succeed, and I am looking forward to that journey that will take us to new levels of growth and success in our enterprise. I deeply regret that not all of us will be able to make it. For those who may not be making that journey with us, I want you to know that it has been my goal from the beginning of this business crisis to avoid layoffs if at all possible. I want to apologize to you for not successfully finding a way to do that. I want to express my personal thanks for the years of service you have put into this company. It will be a painful separation for both of us. We will be doing the best we can to assist you in finding other employment, and I hope one day under better business conditions that some of you will be back with us.

Thank you very much. We appreciate your ongoing hard work and your understanding during this difficult time.

Glossary

Accrued Vacation. Vacation time an employee has accumulated because it has not yet been taken.

Alternative Work Arrangement. A work arrangement that is not a typical 9-to-5 office job. This arrangement involves unique hours, working remotely, and different contractual relationships with the employer, all of which help a company to cut costs, yet at the same time retain the mission-critical skills possessed by certain employees.

COBRA (Consolidated Omnibus Reconciliation Act). A federal law that offers voluntary continued benefit coverage to an employee at a cost to the employee for a specific period of time.

Contracting Arrangements. Work arrangements that change the status of regular employees to a contractual status for part- or full-time work. (See Independent Contractor.)

Early Retirement. An incentive for employees nearing retirement age to leave employment early and retain substantial if not full retirement benefits.

Furloughed Employee. An employee who remains part of the organization but does not work full time or receive full pay. The employee works offsite and is prepared and ready to work once the workload increases.

Hiring Freeze. A decision to suspend all hiring of new employees for a specific time period.

Human Capital. The knowledge and skills an employee possesses that facilitate the company's business practices.

Incentive Compensation. Contingent monetary compensation in addition to one's base salary based on set goals or objectives.

Independent Contractor. An individual who works independently on a project/contract basis for a company. The person supplies his or her own benefits and supplies (e.g., computer), and is responsible for filing his or her tax returns.

Job/Skill Sharing. Reducing staff to part-time status and combining employees to share assignments.

Long-Term Cost Savings. Financial savings a company will achieve in the future by not rehiring employees and having to train them again.

Low-Hanging Fruit. Solutions to problems that are easy to implement and can be done quickly, such as initiating a hiring freeze.

Mandatory Pay Cut. A requirement dictating that all employees take a reduction in pay, including top management.

Mission-Critical Skills. Skills that are critical to an organization to help it achieve its competitive advantage and distinguish itself from competitors.

Older Worker's Benefit Protection Act (OWBPA). A federal law protecting older employees from unfair treatment because of their age.

Outplacement Services. A service offered to employees who were laid off, providing them counseling, coaching, assistance with résumé preparation, and the use of office facilities so they can search for other jobs.

Perquisite Reduction. The decision to remove benefits such as company cars, expense accounts, subsidized lunches, golf club memberships, and so forth to help cut costs.

Real Cost of a Layoff. The many costs that are incurred when an employee is laid off and another is hired, including selection, recruiting, and training costs for the new hires.

Reduction or Suspension of Annual Pay Increases. The decision to cancel all or part of planned pay increases.

Reduction or Suspension of Bonuses and Incentives. The decision to cancel all or part of planned bonuses and incentive payments.

Severance Package. A package offered to an employee when he or she is laid off. This can include a set amount of money, outplacement services, accrued vacation, and benefit continuation.

Short-Term Cost Savings. The immediate savings a company reaps when an employee is laid off, including salary, benefits, perquisites, incentives and bonuses, net of severance costs.

Shorter Work Week. Reduction of staff from a 40-hour to a shorter work week and reduce their salaries proportionately.

Stock Options In Lieu of Pay. Granting employees stock options instead of some part of their current pay or in place of a pay increase.

Strategic Competencies. Competencies (skills) that define how a company will achieve and sustain its competitive advantage in its market or niche. (See Mission-Critical Skills.)

Survivor Syndrome/Guilt. The effect of peers being laid off on an employee retained by the same company. The guilt is often accompanied by fear of future layoffs, excessive work to compensate for the fired employees, a loss of salary, and a need to avoid all risks.

Temporary Assignments. Special assignments for reduced compensation, a specific period (e.g., 3 months) and at a reduced time commitment.

Voluntary Severance. An incentive for employees to voluntarily leave their employment.

Worker Adjustment and Retraining Act (WARN). A federal law that protects employees from plant closings and mass layoffs without notice.

Index

Long-term cost savings, 226
Low-hanging fruit, 226
Loyalty:
    of employees, 38, 182–183
    to employees, 40

M
Management styles, 8
Mandatory pay cuts, 123–124, 226
Mason, Jane, 62
Mass media, 57–59
Meal subsidies, 126
Media, dealing with the, 167–168
Meetings, 57–59, 157
Merit pay, 127–128
Mission-critical skills, 226
Morale, effects of pay cuts on, 124
Motivating others, 19, 23, 35, 185–186
    during crises, 42–43
    and nature of the job, 189
Motorola, 170

N
News, sources of, 56

O
Offsite Net workers, 74–75, 102, 141–143
Older Workers' Benefit Protection Act
    (OWBPA), 120–121, 162, 226
One-on-one discussions (for layoffs), 159
Optimism, 184
Organizational culture, 13, 124, 146, 159,
    170–171, 186
Orientation, employee, 82
Outplacement services, 79, 172, 226
Overtime requirements, 122–123
OWBPA (see Older Workers' Benefit
    Protection Act)

P
Parkland Health & Hospital System, 60, 61
Patience, need for, 38
Pay cuts, mandatory, 14, 123–124, 226
Pay increases, reduction/suspension of annual,
    14, 127–128, 227
Perquisites (perks), reduction of, 14, 125–126,
    226
Perry, Grace, 190–191
Plan(s):
    communications, 55–61
    downsizing, 18

Plan(s) (*Cont.*):
    incentive, 43–44
    recovery, 35
Press releases, 167–168
Productivity, 10
Profitability, 10, 35

Q
QualxServ, 134

R
Real cost of layoffs, 226
Recession of 2001, 12
Recognition, 186–187
Recruitment costs, 82
Replacement employees, costs associated with,
    82–84
Retirement, early, 14, 121–122, 225
Ritz-Carlton, 10
Rumor hotlines, 56

S
Screening costs, 82
Scripted termination messages, 152–153
Second Round (*see* Alternative work
    arrangement[s])
Senior management:
    and criteria for laying off employees, 41–42
    and criteria for retaining employees, 40–41
    getting support of, 18
    level of confidence in, 36
    motivation of employees by, 35–36
    need for change in, 36
    obtaining alignment between employees
        and, 42–43
    optimism of, 184
Separation agreements, sample:
    for more than one individual over 40 years
        of age, 201–203
    for one individual over 40 years of age,
        195–197
Separation packages, 172
Severance, voluntary, 13, 119–121, 227
Severance packages, 79, 80, 164–166, 172, 227
Shell Chemical L.P., 153–154
Shortened work week, 14, 122–123, 227
Short-term cost savings, 227
Skill sharing (*see* Job/skill sharing)
Skills, 8–10
    for alternative work arrangements, 144–146
    focusing on, 43
Special assignments, 15, 216

About the Authors

Fred Crandall, Ph.D., is a founding partner of the Center for Workforce Effectiveness in Northbrook, Illinois, where he serves as a management consultant specializing in compensation and organization issues. He has extensive consulting experience in strategic management, compensation planning, incentive plans, and human resource/organization effectiveness.

Fred is a frequent speaker to domestic and global forums. He is a past president of the Society for Human Resources Management Foundation and an instructor and former course developer for WorldatWork. He is on the editorial review board of *Compensation and Benefits Review* and coauthored the award-winning book entitled *Work and Rewards in the Virtual Workplace: A New Deal for Organizations and Employees.*

Fred has a Ph.D. from the University of Minnesota, a master's degree from the Anderson School of Management at the University of California, Los Angeles, and a bachelor's degree from the University of California, Berkeley. He served as associate professor at the Cox School of Business, Southern Methodist University, Dallas, Texas.

Marc J. Wallace, Jr., Ph.D., is a founding partner of the Center for Workforce Effectiveness in Northbrook, Illinois, where he serves as a management consultant specializing in work force effectiveness, human resource strategy, and compensation. Marc is an internationally recognized expert on rewards and human resource strategy, legal compliance, and compensation. His research findings have been published in over 60 articles and papers in periodicals such as the *Journal of Applied Psychology, Industrial Relations, Compensation and Benefits Review, Decision Sciences, The Journal of Vocational Behavior,* and many others. In 1995 WorldatWork honored Dr. Wallace with the Keystone Contributor Award, recognizing a lifetime contribution to the fields of compensation and human resources.

He has coauthored nine books on management and human resources, including *Organizational Behavior and Performance* (4th ed.), *Administering Human Resources, Compensation Theory and Practice* (2nd ed.), and *Research Based Decisions,* bestselling textbooks that have been used by over 1 million students. He also coauthored *Work and Rewards in the Virtual Workplace: A New Deal for Organizations and Employees.*

Prior to founding the Center for Workforce Effectiveness in 1992, he was professor and Ashland Oil fellow in the Department of Management, College of Business and Economics, University of Kentucky. He holds a bachelor's degree from Cornell University and a master's degree and Ph.D. in industrial relations from the University of Minnesota.

Barbara Ballinger Buchholz is a freelance writer who has written primarily about business, real estate, and design for publications such as the *Chicago Tribune, Crain's Chicago Business, St. Louis Post-Dispatch, The New York Times,* and *House Beautiful.* She has coauthored a dozen books, including *Porches, The Family Business Answer Book: Arthur Andersen Tackles 101 of Your Toughest Questions,* and *Successful Home Building & Remodeling.* She lives in St. Louis, Missouri.

Margaret Crane, a St. Louis, Missouri, journalist, has coauthored several books on business, including *The Family Business Answer Book: Arthur Andersen Tackles 101 of Your Toughest Questions.* Her articles on business have appeared in *Crain's Chicago Business, The New York Times, Money, Family Business Magazine, Your Company Magazine, Inc., Success Magazine,* and the *St. Louis Post-Dispatch* newspaper.